Gunnar Andri Thorisson
www.gunnarandri.is

Ordering Information:
Quantity sales. Special discounts are available on quantity purchases by corporations, associations, and others.

MESSAGE FROM THE MIDDLE OF NOWHERE

Symbol on front cover: Icelandic magical stave Vegvísir,
intended to help people find their right path

Manuscript on front cover:
An Icelandic handwritten letter from 1840

Acknowledgements

When I started writing this book, I had no idea how many individuals would end up contributing to the process and assisting me in this endeavour. The list would extend to several pages if I mentioned every one of them, so I will name just a few. The essential helpers were: Þórir Karl Bragason Celin, for his impressive illustrations and the artwork on the book cover, Hilmar Þorsteinn Hilmarsson, for his patience and professionalism during the layout and design, Snorri Guðmundsson, for his translation work, Heiða Þórðar, for helping me gather my thoughts down on paper and assisting me with tiny but important details like spelling and grammar, showing up every day for many months, Davíð Stefánsson, for his solid editing and translating advice, and Magnús Einarsson for being the one who initially pushed me into this crazy project.

To Aliz Lukács, Einar Victor Karlsson, Aðalheiður Ósk Guðmunds-dóttir, Bjarni Kjartansson and my daughter, Sigurlaug Sara Gunnarsdóttir, I offer my deepest gratitude for being patient concerning my continous rantings about this book. Maria Regina Paiz provided extremely valuable review and proofreading, although all eventual errors are to be attributed to myself. Gunnar Valsson gets special thanks for thinking out loud when I told him that I wanted to write a book. When I expressed my doubts because I was just some guy in the middle of nowhere, he promptly said: "Well, then it will be your message from the middle of nowhere!" And just like that the title of the book was settled!

I also want to express my gratitude for being born in Iceland, this unique place that made it possible for me to write an alternative and unique book about my personal experience.

And finally, the deepest gratitude I offer you, dear reader, for picking up my book and starting to read it. I sincerely hope that my Message From The Middle Of Nowhere will enter your heart and make a difference in your life.

THANK YOU!

① Bláa lónið (Blue Lagoon)
② Þingvellir
③ Keflavík
④ Reykjavík
⑤ Hafnarfjörður
⑥ Kópavogur
⑦ Vestmannaeyjar (Westman Islands)
⑧ Heimaey
⑨ Skagafjörður
⑩ Drangey
⑪ Hofsós
⑫ Höfn í Hornafirði
⑬ Jökulsárlón
⑭ Vatnajökull
⑮ Djúpivogur
⑯ Þvottárskriður
⑰ Litla kaffistofan (a legendary diner close to Reykjavík)

⑱ Hveragerði
⑲ Selfoss
⑳ Skagaströnd
㉑ Hekla
㉒ Bárðarbunga
㉓ Grímsvötn
㉔ Eyjafjallajökull
㉕ Katla
㉖ Siglufjörður
㉗ Svarfaðardalur
㉘ Neskaupstaður
㉙ Viðey
㉚ Snæfellsjökull
㉛ Flateyri
㉜ Súðavík
㉝ Akureyri

Introduction

Message From The Middle Of Nowhere – Fighting Fire And Ice
The Icelandic Viking Philosophy For Conquering The Challenges
Of Business And Life

During the past few years, the same thought has returned to me
each time I've made a mistake. This has especially been the case
during times when I have lost everything or when a significant
life changing or dramatic event has taken place. The thought is
this:

"This is alright, this will only make my book even better."

I believe that this book has important value, and in its pages
you'll find true learning stories and experiences where my
own life is at the forefront. These stories involve mistakes that
I have made, and natural disasters like volcanic eruptions and
avalanches will play a major role. All the stories involve a life
lesson that can be drawn from the experience of a true Viking
born and raised in Iceland, who grew up in poverty but went
on to become the best known salesman in Iceland and ended up
as a sales trainer that has helped thousands of individuals and
corporations to succeed in both business and private affairs.

I believe it's a unique book, since the lessons on life and
the business of sales are intertwined with stories of trolls and
Vikings, elves and superstition, ghosts and fortune–tellers.
You will read stories about getting trapped in the middle of an
avalanche in Iceland, as well as various life changing events
that I experienced while traveling in Africa, Asia, and Europe.

I sincerely hope you enjoy my book and forward its messages
to all the people that are important in your life.

"Our common goal is your success"

CHAPTER 1

When The Eruption Starts, Location Is Everything

All the stories within this book are based on true life experiences and this is the very first one.

I began my career in sales at an early age. A lot has changed since then, but the basic principles remain the same in my personal and professional approach. I believe that the values in all the stories will appeal to everyone who wants to achieve better results in their life dealings and business ventures.

I have worked as a lecturer, consultant and a specialist in communication and sales in Iceland for twenty years, helping both individuals and companies to achieve their maximum sales objectives and true unleashed potential.

It sometimes seems peculiar, even to myself, why I was so interested in making money as a child. During my youth, I only heard negative things when the subject of money came up. This fact is one of the first things I think of when I reflect on my childhood, along with the unforgettable volcanic eruption in the following story that catapulted my career in sales, when I was only six years old!

From an early age, I collected wallets and moneyboxes. Most of these were empty, but that didn't matter to me. My philosophy, even at a young age, was that if I had enough wallets and piggy banks, I would eventually accumulate the money to fill them.

In retrospect, this naive way of thinking seems similar to the law of attraction covered in The Secret. The law of attraction is, of course, a fantastic and powerful principle, but there is one word missing from that particular best-selling book. I would like to add that word into the mix right here:

WORK!

I also learned early on that if you don't ask, then the answer will always be no. As a young boy, I never asked my parents for money, because money simply didn't exist. However, when we had visitors that I knew had enough money, I did not hesitate to approach them by asking a very straightforward, logical and practical question:

"Do you have any money that you aren't using any more?"

This much I had learned: If I wanted money I would just have to make it myself, by asking directly or by attracting the attention of buyers. And, of course, by working hard!

The King, The Troll, The Gnome, And Myself

It was 2 a.m. on January 23, 1973 and the earth started trembling. A large rift had appeared in the ground in the Westman Islands, an archipelago southeast of Reykjavík.

A volcanic eruption had started in Heimaey, the largest of the fourteen islands, hot magma spewing tens of meters into the air. For the first time, a volcanic eruption was taking place in the middle of an Icelandic village.

My heritage lies in the Westman Islands, but while this

dramatic event was unfolding, I was safe and sound, asleep in my bed in Reykjavík, far away from the melting lava and the ongoing confusion in this once peaceful village.

When the volcanic eruption began, the first reaction of a few of the locals was to act upon their growing curiosity and walk right up to the two kilometer-wide expansion rift. From that point they watched the magnificent and natural wonder that soon transformed into a disaster, with absolute amazement, as if they were watching a typical Icelandic New Year's Eve celebration of fireworks and bonfires.

Suddenly it struck them that what they were actually watching was not merely something for their enjoyment and pleasure; they were in fact faced with a life or death situation, the existence and future of their hometown was currently severely at stake. Hot lava ran all over the island, all the way down to the sea, and today it's considered a miraculous blessing that no lives were lost during the eruption.

When The Eruption Starts, Location Is Everything

Only two hours after the eruption initiated, my relatives were safe onboard the rescue boats, heading towards the mainland of Iceland. They had nothing, beside the few things they had been able to hastily put in their pockets and carry away with them. There had been no time to pack anything into bags or suitcases. The circumstances were totally chaotic. They were destitute.

It only took about six hours to evacuate 5,300 people from Heimaey. The key element that saved the lives of the inhabitants of the Westman Island was their swift response rate and how quickly they realized the immense gravity of the situation.

My family from Westman Islands was of course in great

shock, as everyone had lost most of their possessions and some had literally lost everything. Their homes would end up being buried by the dense shower of ash or by the flowing, hot lava.

Therefore, it was somewhat strange for me, at the tender age of six, to stroll around downtown Reykjavík the day following this great natural disaster and do my usual rounds of selling newspapers by calling out to the passing pedestrians:

"Breaking news: Volcanic eruption in Westman Islands!"

The day after my family had lost everything, there I was, selling and shouting out headlines, just to get some pocket money.

An Emerging Career in Sales

So it happened that during these fateful events of 1973, my sales career had already begun. The eruption of the Westman Islands had caused my relatives to lose almost everything, but I, the best-selling paperboy, rewarded myself with chocolate and candy that I purchased with my day's earnings.

Every day after school I would head to downtown Reykjavík to sell newspapers. I wanted to sell outside the national bank, Landsbankinn, because this was considered to be the most profitable location. Incidentally, thirty-five years later that same bank would become one of the largest banks in the world, better known as the bank responsible for the notorious Icesave savings accounts.

Icesave was a giant in the banking sector prior to the economic collapse of 2008, but when I was six years old, Landsbankinn certainly was no giant in my mind. To me, the true giant was Óli 'The Newspaper King', an eccentric little man who sold his newspapers across the street from the bank and had done so for many years.

Óli had claimed this busy corner as his own and no paperboy dared to enter his territory. For a kid like myself, Óli was indeed a big threat and I felt like a pawn in his presence. He was the opposition. He was my nemesis.

Taking On 'The King

Early on in my career I learned that location is key. With my boyish ambition, I saw an opportunity to sell a lot of newspapers because with Óli's location, I would be able to reach a larger crowd. I told some of my fellow paperboys about this idea but they told me it was hopeless. I had no chance of going against 'The King', they would tell me. In fact, I have heard similar phrases numerous times over the years when presenting ambitious ideas. And I'm sure you have too.

Anyway, I gathered my courage, went to the corner and began to sell my newspapers. I had only been there for a short while when Óli began to threaten me and tell me he would turn the police on me if I didn't leave at once. This is my corner, he said angrily. Listening to Óli's threats terrified me, but there was a question to be answered:

Was I going to let fear control me and give up, or was I going to face that fear?

I was fixed on securing for myself the corner across the street from Óli. I was not willing to give up on my dream. There had to be another solution than giving up. Once you begin giving up, you keep giving up. And that is a terrible habit, because first we create habits and then the habit becomes us.

I refused to give up against Óli and I continued stubbornly going downtown to sell newspapers. I started moving closer and closer to the corner next to the Post Office and by doing so, I was able to sell the occasional paper on Óli's territory. My journey towards fortune had started with careful steps in the right direction.

Being able to secure that location, even for a short period of time, did indeed help me to sell papers. I started winning small battles and that made me very proud, even though I had not won the war and the dream had not yet come true.

This is the only way to conquer larger milestones – with many small victories. I have learned that the way to commence and conquer a large project is by taking small steps. Just like Socrates told the traveler that asked him how to get to the top of Mount Olympus:

"Just make sure that every step you take is in that direction."

So, what was I going to do regarding the 'location problem'? The solution had been right in front of me all the time.

The Troll Enters The Scene

There was a man that often stood nearby where this rivalry of Óli and myself took place. He was a giant of a man, much larger than Óli, and he was collecting money for the poor on behalf of the Salvation Army. In Iceland, all trolls or 'tröll' are gigantic, and next to this 'tröll', Óli The King looked like a gnome.

"This is a cool guy," I thought to myself. He looked like a combination of a fairy–tale troll and an Icelandic Viking. I found myself thinking that I needed to get this guy to join forces with me. *What can a gnome like Óli do against someone like him?* I thought to myself.

I went over and talked to the Troll and asked him how the collection was going. He told me it wasn't going well enough, especially considering the importance of the matter.

I told him that I had an idea that was guaranteed to improve his collection and asked him if he would look into it. He smiled and was more than willing to listen. After my explanation, the Troll and I joined forces and he would receive a percentage of my earnings, provided that he would protect me.

The expression on Óli's face, the best-selling newspaper gnome, was certainly not kind when he saw me marching towards him, ready to sell my newspapers, with my new giant friend. Óli didn't give up without a struggle and of course he tried to bully us away. After all, this was his location, but the Troll was very capable of answering back and rightly pointed out to Óli that he didn't own Reykjavík, let alone the public street corners. The tables had now turned and Óli's fear turned out to be uncalled for. We both sold our papers and there was enough business for the both of us.

My confidence soared due to these events and I firmly resolved to become successful. I realized that the Troll would not stand next to me for percentages if I didn't achieve any sales success. I had to deliver for the plan to work, and of course, I wanted to let the Troll benefit from my success since he helped me achieve mine.

At that time, sales took off and I was 'on fire'. I had a burning desire to do well and I felt great. I felt like I possessed more energy than the Westman Island eruption and the Eyjafjallajökull eruption combined.

At the age of six, I was the man!

The First Smell of Success

Ironically, the thoughts I had at that time were not only the naïve thoughts of a young paperboy; these principles are fully valid in real life, no matter where we are situated in the world or in our personal lives.

I went from selling very well to selling extremely well. In a flash, my numbers became really impressive. The pinnacle of my career as paperboy was when I was informed that I had the highest sales figures of all the other paperboys, including Óli 'The King'. I have felt this same feeling later in my career, and there is nothing that compares to it.

At this point I was getting all sorts of personal rewards in the form of chocolate, soft drinks and movie tickets. The gnome wasn't a threat anymore. I had proper money in my wallet and I felt like the King of Sales. It wasn't just about having beaten Óli, the man I had been so afraid of, but also having won this personal victory by reaching my own goal and being successful in my own terms.

This true story has always reminded me that I have to face my fears, whether they appear as trolls or gnomes.

In the story, I benefited from the natural disasters, but of course it's natural to do so. In 2010, numerous travelers became stranded in airports around the world following the eruption of the glacier Eyjafjallajökull. The airlines came to a standstill for days and many travelers lost a fortune, but Icelanders would eventually end up profiting from the eruption. Many tourists worldwide cursed us lavishly while the eruption took place, but a huge increase in tourist bookings and arrivals to the country was evident soon afterwards and continues to this day.

I am proud of the six year old me and how solution–oriented and innovative he was. I have never met a great sales person, entrepreneur or a business manager that thinks like the average Joe and has achieved greatness. It all boils down to this wonderful feeling of victory and the message is simple:

It doesn't matter if you are a kid selling newspapers or the CEO of a large corporation – you can't achieve great success with mediocre thinking.

Messages From The Middle Of Nowhere

– Knowledge can never be taken from you.
– WORK is the magic word.
– If you don't ask the question, the answer will always be no.
– Location is key.
– No one is larger, bigger or greater than you.
– First we make habits and then the habits become us.
– Major milestones are achieved with small victories.
– The solution is often closer than you think.
– Let others benefit from your success if they had a part in it.
– We act outwardly as we feel within.
– If you want to grow, you must face your fears.
– One of the dangers of giving up is
that it might become a habit.
– Don't be afraid to ask for reinforcement when
you need to strengthen your team.

And last but not least:

– The giant in your path can turn into a gnome if you have
a troll on your side.

CHAPTER 2

A Viking Salesman In The Country Of Elves

The Geography of Family

My father came from the Westman Islands, the rural paradise where the catastrophic volcanic eruption took place. Despite the eruption, it is still home to more than 4,000 people today. Puffins (fratercula arctica) have made these islands their main nesting area in Iceland, their estimated population in the Westman Islands reaching 1.1 million couples.

The puffin is a black bird and it's the most common bird in Iceland, totalling around 10 million birds. You will commonly find puffin around the coastal regions and it's estimated that 60% of the world's population nests in Iceland.

Regarding their anatomy and color, black birds in the northern hemisphere are somewhat similar to penguins in the southern hemisphere, but there are only three species to be found on the entire planet.

My mother hailed from Skagafjörður, an area in the northern part of Iceland. This prosperous agricultural area is well known in Iceland for its green pastures, local talents in singing and chanting, and also for the boisterous spirit of the inhabitants, especially the men! Winters in these parts are much heavier in snowfall than in the Westman Islands region and it's the only area in Iceland where you'll find that horses outnumber people, even though, like in the Westman Islands, the human population is similarly around 4,000 inhabitants.

Off The Horse And On Again

For many years, Skagafjörður was the dwelling where I spent the summer with my grandmother on my maternal side. It was here that I learned a multitude of important and valuable life lessons.

One of the things I learned in the fresh air of Skagafjörður is that you are not a horseman unless you have been thrown off your horse, at least once! This was made very clear to me, time and time again.

Echoing this, I have consistently believed and declared that you are not a genuine entrepreneur unless you've failed at least once. The key to this lesson is to always climb right back on and continue your journey. Just as you don't switch horses in the middle of a river, you don't change business partners and co-workers in the middle of a project.

(Where is all this imagery from nature coming from? Personally, I am intrinsically intertwined with Icelandic culture and nature and the Icelandic language is also bursting with beautiful expressions and connections to the harsh but fascinating surroundings. That's why).

Feminism From The Turf House

My grandmother on my maternal side was born in a traditional Icelandic turf house. For the Icelandic nation, it seems like yesterday that we discontinued using that kind of housing. During the 20th century, Iceland transformed dramatically from a turf house society into a society of luxury in a very short timespan. WWII brought about boosting economical effects that played a big role in this. My own family is one of fishermen and farmers, perhaps in fact the entrepreneurs of yore.

You might even claim that this is the fundamental reason for the strength of Icelandic women and how much we have achieved regarding gender equality. For many years, as a general rule, men practiced seamanship in all kinds of dangerous conditions and they frequently put themselves in acute life threatening situations. In Iceland, an old proverb of ancient times is still used to this day: "Sjórinn gefur og sjórinn tekur." The sea giveth, the sea taketh away. Throughout this endurance, it was the women who took care of the homes, the farming and the offspring. Icelandic women had the role of general managers of their households while the men were away providing for the home.

I have also been told that my father's grandmother was the first woman in the Westman Islands who went to sea as a deckhand on a fishing boat and that she did this as a sole provider to her six boys.

The First Female President

It should now be clear to the reader that I am very proud of the inner strength of Icelandic women, but I cannot go on without mentioning that we had the world's first democratically elected female president.

Vigdís Finnbogadóttir served as our president from 1980–1996 and the Icelandic nation is deeply proud of her, both professionally and personally. My favorite aspect is how proud Vigdís is of our ancient Icelandic language and also how she shows a deep and genuine interest in the multiple languages of the world and the interaction of nations through language and culture. In Iceland we have an important institution that is both inspired by and named after Vigdís, The Vigdís Finnbogadóttir Institute of Foreign Languages, and the initiation for its headquarters was accomplished on International Women's Day, March 8, 2015. The institution has become highly appreciated in Iceland and received a formal certification by UNESCO in 2013.

Mom and Dad and The Question of Money

Let's get back to my mother and my father. In all honesty, they were two people that simply were not happy together and I can't say that my upbringing was exemplary. Nonetheless, they taught me numerous good and positive lessons and even today, I strive to keep these closer to me than the negative ones. The negative ones often had to do with money. My father, for example, was constantly professing negative things about money, that it didn't grow on trees, that money was the root of all evil, and so on.

You might be familiar with clichés and utterings of this kind.

Today I know better: Money is neither good nor bad – money is completely neutral.

I have also learned firsthand that money can open doors that have been previously firmly locked. On the other hand, a lack of money has ruined many relationships and families too. Money is always relevant, for each and every one, and you can never earn money unless you sell something: an idea, a product, or a service that you provide.

My parents were divorced when I was 10 years old. By that time, I had already been selling all kinds of small goods from house to house, newspapers and many other items that came my way – and this I did in order to buy myself toys and other desirable items.

The Conflicts of Childhood

Lego was my absolute favorite. I loved to build them and I would totally forget the world while I was at it, especially when my mom and dad were arguing. I'm pretty sure that this Lego obsession of mine was my way of temporarily visiting a different world and fade out the arguments at home.

I can easily and lovingly say that in many ways I never really understood my parents. They lived a very limited and minimalistic life. Neither of them had a driver's license or a car, neither of them had their own apartment and they never traveled abroad (apart from one single exception). As for me, I wore secondhand clothes that my mother had been given in the homes that she cleaned.

We never had dinner at quality restaurants. In recent years, when I have taken my father out to dinner, he has expressed the opinion that it is an extravagant waste of money, since all of the food will eventually end up down the toilet.

Why were my parents the way they were?

I have no idea. Not really. But it is my strong belief that although we are all molded by our upbringing and our environment, we can always induce positive changes within ourselves. It is our own path, our own attitudes that count –

especially towards money. One thing is for certain: Negative attitudes towards money will not bring more money your way.

The thing is this: Since money can be used for security, housing, food, transportation, gifts, or travel, for all of this I cannot believe that money is evil.

I simply can't.

Maybe this is the reason I've managed to experience all of the above – all of the above and more – many times over. Nevertheless, I am still very grateful for my childhood and the parenting that I received, since it became an inspiration to me in the end. We can use a bad childhood experience to justify our loser mentality or we can let it move us towards success and victory, but this is all up to you. If you are an adult, then you and you alone are at the helm.

That Thing That is Bigger Than Us

After my parents divorced, I lived with my mother, but I visited my father regularly. This was partly because my mother needed peace and quiet. She was often very sick, fighting cancer after previously having had one breast removed.

One fateful weekend my mother was hospitalized in a serious condition. I felt anxious and worried, and I never would have imagined that I was about to have the strangest experience of my 11-year-old life.

During the night of February 26th 1978, I lay asleep in the living room at my father's house and my mother appeared to me in a dream. She said she had a message for me and that she wanted to say goodbye. And as soon as she had delivered her message I woke up to a massive earthquake. At first I thought that the house was collapsing, having been heavily influenced by stories of volcanoes and earthquakes from my father and his brothers. Incidentally, the fear of a volcanic eruption is something that the Icelandic people always live with, at least subconsciously.

This was not the case, however. This was no natural disaster but another kind of wonder of the world. The noise came from Marinó, my father's brother, and a strong giant of a man that could easily have won the Strongest Man In The World competition, had he ever tried. Marinó had a habit of teasing me by hooking his finger under my belt and hauling me to the ceiling to 'toughen me up'.

And there he was, banging on the windows where I was sleeping, making me think that my mother had brought an earthquake with her. Marinó had been sent to bring me the news of my mother's passing. He knew that I was alone asleep inside the house, but since I hadn't answered the doorbell after his numerous attempts he had worried that something was wrong.

After a while I calmed down from his thunderous banging, but the fact was I had already known about my mother's passing. She had appeared to me that night. She had said goodbye to me and given me the message she had wanted to leave behind. It was after this experience that I became convinced that there is something out there that is much bigger and more significant than we can imagine.

Influential Elves

It is often said that Icelanders believe in the most incredible things, elves and fairies, for example. And it's true – elves are a common phenomenon in Icelandic culture and many contemporary Icelanders still believe in their existence. A great example of this is the street Álfhólsvegur, where I once lived with my grandmother. The literal translation of the street name is 'Elf Hill Road' because when it was constructed the plan was to remove a small knoll that some people said had been the home of an elf family. During the construction, the contractor got into all kinds of inexplicable trouble with his machinery and the delays were endless and costly. Finally, to avoid any more trouble, it was decided that the road would simply be detoured, and today this small area has an official protection as a domicile for elves.

For me, it serves as a great example of how strong our folklore is amongst Icelandic people, right up to this day. We believe.

And although these examples aren't directly related, I have without a doubt witnessed that some forces exist that I cannot explain with logic.

One thing is certain. I knew which news Marinó was bringing, even though I would never have imagined, when I drifted off to sleep, that my mother would die that night. I am convinced that the power of the mind is limitless and I wouldn't be surprised if it became possible to learn telepathy in the near future. Even send a message with your mind, but that's another story.

Life shapes us and everyone receives his or her dose of disappointment and suffering. I consider myself a lucky man, even though I've lost many close relatives and friends across the great divide. This has taught me to enjoy life to the fullest and live in the now. Like Óskar, one of my best friends who passed away much too early in his life, used to say: "Life is now, enjoy it." For me, this has over time been translated into my own saying that is a personal mantra of mine:

Time is indeed a limited resource.

A New Life With 'Amma og Afi'

When one door closes another opens. This is exactly what happened when I moved in with my grandmother and grandfather at Álfhólsvegur after my mother died. They worshipped me and everything around me was kept in order. Food was always served punctually at the table, both lunch and dinner, breakfast and evening refreshments. They stressed the importance of eating healthy food if you wanted to stay energetic and maintain full concentration, and what characterized my grandmother's cooking were the old Icelandic traditions.

We often had 'svið' (a smoked sheep head, cut in half) and 'harðfiskur', our delicious wind-dried and salted fish, still very popular amongst Icelanders and also much appreciated by tourists arriving in Iceland, who sometimes refer to it as Viking Snack. Skyr was a popular item at my grandmother's house, a delicious Icelandic cultured dairy product, similar to strained yogurt. It has been a part of Icelandic cuisine for over a thousand years and it's traditionally served cold with milk and a topping of sugar or a handful of fresh Icelandic blueberries. The average life expectancy of an Icelander is 83 years and it's even higher amongst women. It may be because of the smoked sheep heads, but it probably has more to do with our special elixir, lýsi, which is super healthy fish oil.

We ate a variety of fish, sometimes charr and salmon that we caught ourselves during the summer. Meat was sometimes served, but not very frequently. We ate mostly lamb.

In Iceland, the farmers breed the sheep exclusively for meat, although we also use the wool in different ways. The Icelandic lamb has a wonderful 'game' flavor, since the animals graze on fresh grass and wild plants while they are roaming wild during the bright, Icelandic summer.

Come to think of it, no one seemed to be overweight in

those days, yet we were constantly eating and drinking! Maybe we only started having trouble with obesity after the rise of the fast food business and the candy business, and when we stopped using our bodies for work or exercise? It really isn't complicated. If you eat healthy, and work out, you stay in shape. My grandmother was absolutely correct in her view: Eat healthy and frequently during each day.

Grandma's Strength And Philosophy

My grandmother was a solid and strong woman. Having transformed her life after my grandfather's death she moved to the city and remarried. I always looked up to her and she remains one of my strongest role models. She always spoke to me like a peer and in an objective manner, she always listened attentively to what I had to say and she respected my beliefs. She gave me time, love and respect.

Without a doubt, this is the main reason why I feel it's completely natural that people listen to what I am saying, be it the President or an important CEO, or just your average Joe. My grandmother taught me to talk sharply but efficiently and also to listen and pay full attention (you know, the principle of having two ears but only one mouth).

She also taught me to read into the lines when people talk, and not to take it personally when people disagree with me. I learned a great many things from my grandmother, and also from my step-grandfather. They were honest, old-fashioned individuals who taught me almost everything I know today, and I will forever be indebted to them.

In fact, they gave me everything. So many people are shy or dare not express themselves. I am convinced that they simply didn't get proper encouragement during childhood, creating a fractured self-image. We behave in accordance with how we feel and for this reason we must speak kindly to ourselves from the inside. If we do this, we find the strength to take action, without making excuses.

Grandma was an avid reader and a genuine entrepreneur, without knowing or realizing it. In fact, I think genuine entrepreneurs don't waste time or energy pondering whether or not they are entrepreneurs or not. They simply carry on with their actions. No doubt my grandmother was clueless to the fact that she was a remarkable woman. She was too busy founding women's coalitions and charities to consider that.

"Read, Gunnar Andri!"

One of grandma's many important messages was:

"To keep your head sharp you *must* read! You need to keep your head in practice, the same way you need to constantly play chess to improve your game or at least stay good! And the same goes for your body!"

I listened to this advice and still hold on to it, especially the reading part. During these years I had two favorite categories. I read self-help books, such as *The Power of Positive Thinking* by Norman Vincent Peale, but I also read the *Collected Icelandic Folktales* by Jón Árnason, with stories that were full of magic, witchcraft, ghosts and magic runes.

Personally I like it if I can find an interesting story and some wisdom from the same story or the same book. Maybe this is why I structured this book of mine the way I did? Maybe it has something to do with combining the right and left hemispheres? Some people want stories and others want facts. Hopefully my book presents the best of both worlds.

Bobby Fischer

My grandmother taught me so many things in my life and some of the strongest messages I have included in this book have come directly from her. She and her husband were old-school people who taught me how to play a solid game in both bridge and chess. Now, that's what I call proper life training! Bridge and chess are for everyone, no matter how old you are. The best thing about chess is that you need to plan many moves ahead; nothing is over until it's over, and one final lethal strike near the end may leave you dead. Checkmate, game over. Anyone can play, but you must outsmart your opponent in every move to win.

I often think about Bobby Fischer, that genius of a man that many people claim was the greatest chess player of all times. At age 15, he was World Chess Champion. He played eight World Champion tournaments and won them all.

My grandmother and her husband were huge fans of Fischer, ever since his legendary victory over Boris Spassky in Reykjavík 1972, and he was frequently mentioned around the dinner table. Later on, in March 2005, Bobby Fischer moved to Iceland after having being granted Icelandic citizenship. This grand master of chess died from kidney failure in January 17th 2008 and is buried in Selfoss, a town close to Reykjavík, where the recently established Bobby Fischer Center houses memorabilia from his career.

The Salesman And The Toilet Paper

When I was 12 years old I took a huge step when I applied for a job at KRON Supermarket on Álfhólsvegur in Kópavogur, a town close to Reykjavík. My job description? Delivering groceries to people in the neighborhood, running around on an old, black bike with a special delivery frame in the front. It sounds charming, right? It sure does, but it was a heavy bike and riding it in the snow and on slippery roads during the winter was very difficult.

Often the snow was so heavy that I couldn't use the bike and instead I went on foot in all kinds of weather, in biting frost on icy roads, carrying heavy shopping bags, full of groceries. But I always showed up and gave this job everything I had, living by what I later realized was a motto of always being the best version of yourself, no matter what job or task you are doing.

These times were highly instructive, although they were also exceptionally hard on me. It was during this period in my life, around 12 years old, when I first remember having the idea of starting my own sales school. This pre–teen dream was to become a reality about 18 years later, when I founded the SGA Sales School.

This wild idea came to me one day in the grocery store were I worked. I was doing a shift in the fresh meat section and I saw this salesman type of a guy enter the store and stroll through, super full of confidence. He asked for the store manager, claiming he was selling toilet paper. The first thing the manager did, of course, was ask about the price. The salesman gave him the price, and immediately the manager turned him down, saying that the product was too expensive.

"Really? How so?" asked the salesman.

"It costs more than the standard toilet paper," replied the manager.

"Yes, yes indeed," said the salesman, before grabbing one roll of toilet paper and slamming it on the meat scale right in front of me. The numbers didn't lie; his roll was much heavier than your standard roll. The quantity outweighed the price and my store manager instantly put in a large order with the salesman. He had argued that this toilet paper was not more expensive than the regular one, and he was right.

That Single Moment That Changes Your Life

In this memory I see myself standing there with a light bulb above my head, an innocent boy, surrounded by fresh meat and these two adults doing business. Something started to stir inside me and I began to ask myself: "Is there such a thing called a 'sales school'? Can you learn to become an outstanding salesman?"

Just imagine! A complete stranger walks into my life, completely unaware of the influence he is having on my future and me! This has always amazed me and has reminded me, always, that each and every one of us can become a huge influencing factor in other people's lives, without even knowing it.

After endless lectures and constant sales seminars for small and large groups for 20 years, I know for a fact that I have become an influencing factor in a few lives (I wonder how many!) There is no way to know for sure! Up until now I have been delivering my message mainly to Icelanders, a message I now want to deliver to many more people in this ever–shrinking global marketplace that the world has become.

Always Think Big!

I encourage you to think big. Often the effort is the same, but the glitch is that our own doubts often grip us. But your dreams can easily become your reality; that is to say, if you make sure that the fierce flame inside you is never extinguished. Negative thoughts can kill your spirit and lead you to think about your own potential failure. Turn it the other way around and think instead: "What if I reach my goals or the big dream comes true? How will my life become then?"

Unnecessary worries should also be put to rest. They often stem from lack of action, which can easily be changed with a simple action plan. The best thing is that the minute you take a single step towards your dreams or goals, everything changes. Just remember that if your projects and approaches tend to cause people to express their critical opinion … you are probably doing somehing right!

My opinion is this: If you read this book and don't talk about it afterwards, either in a positive or negative manner, then I will have failed. All strong messages should be somewhat polarizing. Nothing happens if nothing is put forward, and if you disagree with my message, at least it will serve as a catalyst for your own processing of opinions.

Everyone Is Selling, All The Time

Now, back to the super–salesman with the toilet paper and my epiphany regarding a sales school. I really would have liked to study the art of successful salesmanship during those early years of mine. But I soon realized that no 'sales school' was to be found in Iceland, despite the obvious fact that you have to sell stuff if you want your business to make money, and also despite the fact that 'selling' is a big factor in every person's existence.

This inner struggle often seems to hinder us in life. We somehow feel that we don't deserve the money that can flow in our direction. Everyone has his or her own fight, internally, socially, towards family members, friends, even nature. Some fight in all these areas. But we always have to sell ourselves the important idea that it's useful for us to become more qualified in human interactions and to be able to lure out this important, simple word from other people:

Yes.

Through the day we are constantly selling ideas. We sell ideas to our children and our children sell ideas to us. And in my opinion, children are often the greatest salesmen.

Why?
First of all: They don't take your 'no' personally.
Second: They are genuine and honest.
Third: They wait for the right opportunity to make their request.
Fourth: They never give up.

During childhood, when someone tells you 'maybe', you actually hear: Yes.

But for grown-ups, we very quickly translate the word 'maybe' into: No.

When does this change of attitude happen in life, and why? I haven't figured out the exact timing of the change, but you could describe it as 'learned hopelessness'. We have tried so many different things in different ways that we learn to give up. To make things worse, the people that are closest to us often want to protect us from disappointment and suffering when we don't reach our goals and fulfill our dreams, and they tend to do this by discouragement. In a way, and all too often, people are bringing us down to their own level of confidence and lack of drive.

In our younger years we allow ourselves to dream and we freely tell people about our hopes, desires, and longings. This all gets smothered along the way to adulthood.

You might be reluctant to believe in fairy creatures, trolls or elves, but there truly exists a species called 'dream-thieves'. They are the people constantly trying to kill your dreams, and you should avoid them at all cost.

Don't ever give up. Never. Simply strive to learn the rules, just like when you learn to play chess. Practice, because that's how you become perfect. Turn your defeats into victories and remember: you can use your chains to forge a sword.

Messages From The Middle Of Nowhere

– Your methods and attitudes in certain actions are most likely similar in other actions. Manifest an ambition in the smaller actions too.

– Don't take the NOs personally.

– When one door closes, another door opens, and sometimes many do at the same time.

– Something exists that is grander than all of us, a phenomenon we cannot fully explain.

– Words are full of spells, so be careful how you talk about yourself and other people.

– If you fall from your horse, climb back on it and carry on.

– Always keep reading to keep your head in shape.

– Anything can be learned.

– Money is not good or bad. Money is neutral.

– The core of worries is lack of action.

– Practice makes perfect.

– Love, time, and respect are our greatest gift to our children.

– Don't switch horses in the middle of the river.

– Negative attitudes towards money will not bring more money your way.

– We can use a bad childhood experience to justify our loser mentality, or let it move us towards success and victory.

– Time is indeed a limited resource.

– Life is now, enjoy it.

– Always be the best version of yourself, no matter what job or task you are doing.

– Every one can become a huge influencing factor in other people's lives, without even knowing it.

And last but not least:

– The sea giveth, the sea taketh away.

CHAPTER 3

From Motivated Fool
To Master Salesman

"Life isn't always fair, get used to it and move on"

Starting Out At The Farm

I was happy to stay with my grandmother and step-grandfather, even though accepting my mother's death was a hard thing to do at the time. My relationship with my father was sporadic so the only option I had was to accept this unchangeable situation and move on with my life.

So, life went on. During the summers I always spent some time in Skagafjörður where my grandmother and her husband had a piece of land and a cottage. It was only a few minutes' walk to the farm of my mother's brother, and it was there that I learned how work could build your character.

Although I was just a kid, I was given various jobs at the farm. That was simply the way of things at this time and this place. I soon realized that you had to earn your keep and that nothing was free in this world. I would herd the calves to the farm in the afternoon and herd the sheep long distances into the pastures in the valley. During each summer I would, like most people in the area, overexert myself cutting grass and managing the hay that was fed to the livestock during the winter, and since this is the most important job on an Icelandic farm we would continue throughout the evenings and often into the night when the weather would allow it. Of course this was possible because of the long hours of sunlight in Iceland. During the summer months, especially June and July, the sun practically never sets, so we have almost full daylight during the night, too.

So, it was a race against time and weather because we had to bring the hay into the barn before it would start raining once again. During these long hours the grown-ups would tell us many stories from Skagafjörður about elves and trolls and the like.

Living Legends In The Icelandic Nature

One of the stories I will never forget is that of Drangey Island. Drangey has steep sea cliffs and sits majestically in the midst of Skagafjörður Bay. The island is the remnant of a 700,000-year-old volcano, mostly made of volcanic tuff, forming a massive rock fortress. My grandmother told me the story, and it goes something like this:

Two night–trolls, a man and a woman, were traversing Skagafjörður at night along with their cow. The rays of daybreak were suddlenly upon them and, as a result of the exposure to daylight, all three were turned into stone.

Today, Drangey represents the cow and the rock formation 'Kerling' (supposedly the female giant, the name means 'Old Hag') stands to the south of it. Karl (the male giant) used to be located to the north of the island, but he disappeared many years ago.

Of course I believed this story without doubting it! It was somehow a part of the environment and culture and all the stories about trolls made perfect sense. But Grýla and Leppalúði are without question the most famous trolls in Iceland, even today. This is because they are the mom and dad of the thirteen Icelandic Santa Clauses.

Thirteen Santa-Clauses ... And a Christmas Cat?

Yes, it's true. We do have thirteen Santa Clauses in Iceland!

According to Icelandic myth, the trolls Grýla and Leppalúði have thirteen 'jólasveinar' or 'yuletide lads'. Grýla and Leppalúði are terribly frightening, ugly creatures. At Christmas time, Grýla is said to steal children that have been naughty during the year (she's gonna find out who's naughty or nice!). Through the centuries Grýla has been a popular way to make children behave, but despite numerous legends and stories about Grýla and her exploitations she never seems to get her hands on any children. For one reason or another, they have either been very well behaved or they've simply managed to escape.

Our Icelandic Christmas Cat also deserves a mention here. He is the huge house cat of Grýla and Leppalúði and, according to legend, he eats children who don't wear at least one new piece of clothing during Christmas. This myth lead to a tradition, still alive today, where everyone is given a new piece of clothing before Christmas, so that no one will 'get caught by the Christmas Cat'.

For me, it seems remarkable that to this day it is frowned

upon to wear used clothes on Christmas. Simply because of this old myth, we feel pressed to buy new clothes. It is proof of the power of the words spoken to us, and the words we tell ourselves.

The result of our childhood Icelandic tales is therefore ominous: *Get new clothes or the Cat will eat you ... and behave well all year or Grýla will eat you!*

It's the Boogeyman, times two!

Grýla Should Only Be A Myth

The fact is that we are accustomed to scaring ourselves into action, or inaction. So many adult individuals don't live their own life, but instead copy the lives of their parents. *What kind of Grýla do you inflict upon yourself?* Who will come eat you if you don't behave, or if you don't do things the way you are 'supposed' to? Who will come after you? Society? Your friends? Your parents or other relatives?

My message is clear: Grýla is a myth. Only you keep her alive inside yourself. This life is your own life. You should live it fully in any way that pleases you.

We receive messages from our surroundings and the people in our lives, right from our birth and throughout our entire lifespan. This does not mean that all these messages are true. A large part of adult life has to do with screening the messages that society wants to send us.

The Value Of The Work Ethic

The time at the farm taught me many things that would later become valuable to me, such as the importance of working hard and finishing assignments on time. My story is not unique. Throughout the years, many business owners and managers have expressed how employees who have been raised on farms or in the small villages of Iceland have a superior work ethic than those who have been raised in the city, which is why they tend to get raises and promotions more frequently. People from the countryside are in general more punctual and more dedicated to their jobs.

Whether this generalization is true or not, it seems obvious that self–discipline and a healthy work ethic must be taught by example. Fortunately, I received this kind of input during my childhood, and self–discipline and resilience were ingrained in me thanks to my outstanding role models.

When I began working in the fish–freezing plant at Hofsós, close to my grandmother's house, I quickly started earning some extra money due to my hard work and extra efforts, which were a direct result of the message I had received earlier when working on the farm for no salary at all.

At 14 I bought myself a small motorbike, the fanciest one you could buy in Iceland at the time. I paid for it in cash and thus achieved something that my parents never had: I owned a motorized vehicle! My piggy bank contained ample cash for the motorbike, I was really proud of it, and it always came with me to Skagafjörður during the summers.

Origins Must Never Be Forgotten

Hofsós is a small village in the eastern region of Skagafjörður, one of the oldest commercial spots in Iceland, dating back to the 15th century. Although only 200 people live there today, it's a lively society. Apart from its stunning nature, the villagers are particularly proud of The Icelandic Emigration Center, which is both a museum and a research center for the emigration of Icelanders during 1870–1914, when numerous Icelanders left to settle in North–America, mostly in the northern part of the U.S. and in Canada. It's estimated that between 15,000 and 20,000 Icelanders emigrated during this period, amounting to 20–25% of the total population.

One of Hofsós' gems must also be mentioned: an outdoor swimming pool facing the Atlantic Ocean to the north with a spectacular view over the fjord and Drangey Island, the island with the trolls in my grandmother's stories. I don't visit Hofsós too often, but I still try to do it every once in a while for the sole reason that we should never forget where we came from. We need that acknowledgement in order to be able to know where we are going.

"How About A Career In Butchery?"

One thing leads to another. I started working in a meat processing plant and, for a while, I planned on studying the art of butchery. I imagined that it was a decent way of being able to work at a store, which was my 'dream' at that point in my life.

In addition to working in the store, I worked extra shifts at a local hamburger joint. I worked hard at both of these jobs, intent on becoming a salesman or a businessman of some sort.

I believed that I was already a fantastic salesman. I mean, I had conquered Óli, The Newspaper King! I had also been very successful at selling meat to the local housewives, as evidenced by their overstocked freezers.

First Failure Of The Motivated Fool

The truth is that I wasn't born a salesman, no more than anyone else. I had reached the age of 17 and yearned for a real sales job. So, I placed an ad in the local newspaper. An older gentleman soon contacted me and asked me to meet him at his bakery. He wanted to know if I would be able to sell his products to grocery stores, cafeterias, canteens and other locations, and maybe even do some marketing for the bakery itself. Of course I accepted his offer, I sure was up to the challenge and I agreed on a particular percentage that sounded great to me. To put it simply: I was super excited and 100% positive.

Off I went, catalogue, sample products and price list in hand. The people I met with didn't object to the prices and seemed pleased with the products. But still, for some reason, I didn't sell one item. I didn't know the rules and somehow played the 'game' incorrectly. I was checkmate. And today I know why.

Being positive doesn't do the trick on it's own. The sales industry today is full of people I usually refer to as 'motivated fools'. Let's say that you arrive in Iceland, full of positive attitude. Without a map that indicates where you are currently located and where you should be heading, you could walk around Reykjavík in circles, back and forth, without ever finding me.

You would find yourself in the middle of nowhere. At age 17, that was my current location. Nowhere.

Mapping Is Key

Mapping is the key. Wherever you are located, even though you feel like you are in the middle of nowhere, I am utterly convinced that you can achieve success and realize your wildest dreams. It's simple: You must first figure out what you want, then seek out the necessary assistance or help in the form of education, courses, books, seminars, or lectures, and last of all, you map out where you want to be going!

In other words:

1. You need the right attitude.
2. You need the right knowledge.
3. You need to take action, without fearing failure.

This was exactly what I did after my initial failure as a young salesman.

I realized that I was the reason for my failures. I felt a strong desire to learn everything that was to be learned in the sales and marketing industry. I wanted to learn how to play the game. But I soon found out that a sales school simply didn't exist in Iceland and even sales seminars were scarce.

Starting To Learn The Game

The fact was that during those years the Icelandic business scene hadn't evolved very much. Still, I found a seminar that sounded promising: one by Dale Carnegie. Excited, I showed up with my friend Sigurður. We still remain great friends to this day, and he is a part of The Turbo Gang, a group of eight guys who have remained close friends for over 40 years. Once a month we meet at a landmark fish restaurant in Reykjavík, each one sitting in the same seat during all these years. The Turbo Gang is by far one of the most valuable assets in my life.

I learned many useful things during the Dale Carnegie seminar. At the time, the admittance fee was sky-high, especially for a 17 year old kid who was paying his own way. Intuitively, however, I knew this truth:

Quality resonates longer than price.

I am still, to this day, reaping the benefits of that expensive investment in the 17-year-old Gunnar Andri. And, it matches my belief that whatever your position is in this world, you should always keep investing in yourself, your knowledge and your skills. I've kept investing in my learning throughout the years, and it has always helped me immensely, especially when I've had to take some heavy blows in life that I will discuss in the following chapters.

Knowledge is an asset that can never be taken from you. Or, as the saying goes: "If you want to earn more, you have to learn more."

The Success Begins

So there I was, a failed salesman at the age of seventeen. It would have been easy to give up on my dream after my failed attempt at the bakery. And maybe I would have given up, had it not been for my friend Engilbert, who approached me shortly afterwards and said:

"I have a sales job and I think it's perfect for you."

He was adamant about meeting in private to discuss the job in more detail and I remember the whole incident vividly. He told me that he had found a sales position where you could make real money. He mentioned some key figures and my head literally went dizzy. I had never heard of such figures for a sales job! He had certainly gotten my attention, and my interest was aroused.

Then he added:

"It isn't the most fancy sales job, Gunnar Andri. It's not for everyone. And the reason I came to you is because the job is absolutely 'for winners only'."

My curiosity was full blown, and then he finally told me that this was a door–to–door job selling books. Hard work around the whole country in all weathers and conditions, visiting all the small towns and farms in Iceland. He added that many people who had attempted this had given up, but those that stayed on could be in for some serious amounts of money.

It has to be added, in this context, that Icelanders are avid readers and ours is a book-loving nation. Literature has been a large part of our identity and even today we publish an inordinate amount of books per capita each year, for a population of only 330,000 people.

Because of this fact, I was eager to do the job and immediately said YES! Engilbert and I went to the owner of the book company, who welcomed me and seemed to like me. He laid out a set of principles that I was to follow. One of these principles has remained with me to this day. He said: "The day you lose your self–respect and your self–confidence it's time to pack up and leave. Everything is always up to you." Having pondered this over the years, I have come to formulate my own philosophy:

"It doesn't matter what you do, just aim to become the best in your business."

With these guiding principles in my system, I started my debut as a book salesman. It was a rainy, windy night. And it didn't go well.

Where Do You Go From Zero Sales?

I didn't sell a single book that first night, and the disappointment was enormous. But after that, something happened. I was filled with newfound enthusiasm and a competitive attitude, and I simply wasn't ready to accept that I wasn't able to sell books like the other salesmen. I didn't express these feelings to Engilbert or the others, but something was boiling deep down inside of me, some kind of force that was ready to explode into an influence on my potential customers.

The very next night I broke the sales record of the company!

How? What had happened? Well, I used a logical and sensible approach. I mainly tried to sell the books that I was genuinely interested in; the books that I had read myself and could talk about from my heart and with solid and genuine enthusiasm.

The best example of this is The Icelandic Sagas. They are considered unique amongst medieval literature and Iceland's most valuable contribution to the global culture, even to this day. The Sagas are secular stories where the core theme has to do with the honor of early Iceland settlers. They are often full of conflicts and disputes, revenge playing a big role, since it was the duty of men to revenge the wrongdoings against their family and honor. Women play a key role in these sagas, either by fueling revengeful acts or by calming things down. Many of these key characters remain strong icons within the Icelandic culture.

So, it was partly because of The Icelandic Sagas that I reached my epiphany: *When you are selling something, the best way is to do it from the heart.* This is equally true when you are 'selling' an idea to your spouse, your child, or your friends. Some people always speak from their heart, while others speak from other body parts that I prefer not to mention.

The Imitation Game

So, I started to inspect other salesmen who were achieving success. I analyzed them to find out what they were doing differently, and soon I started copying their techniques and making them my role models. Very soon I started to sell as much as these salesmen and even more, which goes to show that when it comes to marketing, certain parameters don't really matter. Whether you are old or young, red-haired or brunette, left-handed or right-handed, the market is a neutral zone, which means that you will reach success if you behave in a successful manner.

And when I had become more successful in sales than those role models of mine, I simply found new ones to examine.

These were certainly influential times for me as a salesman; it was some hard schooling, but all in all it was very beneficial. Being a door-to-door book salesman in Iceland didn't only demand that you excel in your interactions and behaviors, you also had to have tremendous self-discipline in order to venture into the turbulent weather conditions that our harsh country often offers. I had never been abroad when I started my career and my only frame of reference was that winters were dark and summers were bright and that you were always forced to make a great effort in everything you did.

Traveling from place to place during the winter was tough, and conditions were often daunting. But ironically, although bad weather was tough to endure, that's when the sales skyrocketed! After the entire inner struggle, using strong self-discipline to enter the storm, I would meet potential customers at full power.

During nice weather, of course, going out on a sales trip was a breeze, but people would be more reluctant to spend time listening to a sales pitch. During crappy weather, people were more often at home and they had nothing else to do than to listen to a sales pitch.

No Always Means No, But You Can Still Be Selling!

I learned many vital lessons during this book sales period. 'The number of nos doesn't matter; it's the number of yeses that count'. This important principle is always valid and I learned it from from Guðmundur, one of my veteran colleagues. He once told me that he decided to count his nos on a 14-day sales trip. According to him, all in all the nos added up to a staggering 4,384, which seemed unbearable! But the fact remains that he managed to sell books for over 40,000 dollars!

I had to learn this tough lesson the hard way: When you knock on people's doors you have an 80–90% chance of receiving a NO right away. However, if you soon get people chatting, you have already turned the ship around, and then the odds of closing the deal become 80–90%.

Many of our most renowned businessmen started working as delivery boys or door-to-door salesmen. For example, Björgólfur Thor Björgólfsson, the first Icelander to be included on the Forbes magazine's list of the world's wealthiest people, started out by offering freshly picked potatoes door-to-door.

I actually think it's a valuable asset to have learned at a young age not to take the NO personally. Of course I have no idea how often I have received a NO, and even its more forceful alternative: "NO WAY!" But taking this personally will only cause you harm. Every achiever in the world has stumbled and fallen. Does it matter? Absolutely not. Just keep a sharp and clear vision on your future, stay focused and keep moving. The opera ain't over till the victory is yours.

Big In Japan

After having sold quite a number of books, I found myself cruising in my car with Halldór, a childhood friend of mine. He told me about this Japanese girl living in Tokyo; they were pen pals and he was thinking of visiting her. I got really excited; naturally, because I had never even been abroad. We decided to take the plunge together and drove directly to a travel agency downtown.

There we bought our one-month trip to Japan, and take-off was just a few weeks away. This was my first trip, going from a country with 300,000 people to another country with over 127 million people. When I think back, although the figures themselves are forgotten, I remember thinking that for this trip I could have bought myself a fancy Mercedes. Of course, there are no regrets. The memories will always live on, and doing something like this is a kind of a self-investment because when you look back on your life you should embrace what you did and not regret what you did not.

The stories from Japan could fill many pages of this book, but I will limit myself to telling you just one very unlikely story of something that happened in Tokyo.

"I'm From Iceland, Where Are You From?"

We were speechless by the number of people because we had never seen anything like it. All the trains, everywhere and at all times, were packed like a tin of sardines and we were staying at a friend of Halldór's pen pal in an apartment that was barely 30 sqm. Halldór and I were strolling through the crowded streets of Tokyo when I decided to approach a Japanese girl in the middle of the street, by saying to her:

"Hi, I'm from Iceland, where are you from?"

She looked at me like she had seen a ghost or an elf, and responded:

"Oooh ... Iceland? So, do you know a girl called Unnur?"

I was equally as shocked as she was. How was it possible, in this city of millions, that I would approach a random person who happened to know someone from Iceland?

"Yes, I said. We know a girl called Unnur. We are actually invited to a party at her house in a few days when we return back home."

And what do you know? We were both referring to the same Icelandic girl called Unnur! It turned out that the Japanese girl was Unnur's pen pal and this story ended with us bringing Unnur all sorts of gifts from her Japanese friend!

Like I always say: "If you never ask, you will never know."

This incredible incident was echoed a few days later when we accompanied Halldór's pen pal to her American College. As we walked down the hall, I popped my head into one of the classrooms and again I said:

"I'm from Iceland, where are you from?"

An older gentleman, sitting by his desk, seemed genuinely astonished. He was a short fellow with gray hair and glasses, looking like a professor. Before him was a pile of stacked books. Then he shouted out:

"Iceland … ooooohh … Iceland!"

We were a bit hesitant, but he motioned us to his desk and showed us the books in front of him, in Danish, Finnish, Norwegian, and Swedish, and finally he enthusiastically showed us a book of Icelandic folktales that he had been studying.

He asked me if I could read the book, which of course I could do, even though it was written in Old Icelandic, but Icelandic is one of the oldest preserved languages in the world. He explained to us that he was a language teacher and that he was fascinated with Icelandic because of how little our language had changed over the centuries. He also liked the fact that there were some letters that were not found in the English alphabet, and even some letters that were only used in the Icelandic language.

So, during my short stay in Japan, I ended up dictating some Icelandic folktales onto cassettes that were later used in that American College in Tokyo.

I really enjoyed my time in Japan, getting to know this alternative culture and ways of life that were totally different from the Icelandic way. I had always been content in Iceland with all the darkness of winter and the harsh winds and cold rain. I had never missed the sun or the warmth, simply because you cannot miss a thing that you have never experienced. But my trip to Japan managed to broaden my perspectives and made me realize how little I knew about the world.

It probably created in me the urge to move on – to start exploring the world and widening my horizon. This urge has never left me and it has kept me going ever since.

Messages From The Middle Of Nowhere

– No one is born a fantastic salesman, but it can easily be learned.

– The market is a neutral zone, which means that you will reach success if you behave in a successful manner.

– Sell a product that you know well.

– Deliver your message straight from your heart.

– Know your location and where you are heading.

– Be prepared to apply self-discipline.

– The nos don't matter, it's the yeses that count.

– If you never ask, you will never know.

¬– You can influence and encourage your own 'luck'.

– You can't miss something that you have never experienced.

– Life isn't always fair, get used to it and move on.

– Always keep investing in yourself, your knowledge and your skills.

– Knowledge is an asset that can never be taken from you.

– It doesn't matter what you do, just aim to become the best in your business.

– When you are selling something, the best way is to do it from the heart.

And last but not least:

– What kind of Grýla do you inflict upon yourself? Who will come eat you if you don't behave? Grýla is a myth. Only you keep her alive inside yourself.

CHAPTER 4

Stuck BetweenTwo Avalanches

"A Mobile Phone? Are You Crazy?"

It was a typical winter's day with snow and a light drizzle. Some co-workers and I, Óli, Sveinbjörg and Sigurður, were heading for a sales trip through the eastern fjords of Iceland and the weather forecast wasn't looking good. Óli suggested that we buy a mobile phone for safety. Mobile phones were a real novelty at the time, but I still liked the idea. I remember thinking that the only person in Iceland that had a mobile phone was our beloved and eccentric veteran news reporter Ómar Ragnarsson, who traveled through the outskirts of Iceland on his jeep and his small airplane.

I knew a guy who owned a mobile phone store, since I used to deliver groceries to his house for many years when working for KRON as a kid. He was clearly still fond of me because he gave us a huge discount and therefore it was easier for us to justify this kind of expenditure to ourselves. We shared the cost, as the amount was certainly substantial for a couple of young salesmen.

The phone itself was a Mitsubishi 'phone station', weighing a number of kilos. Our friends and colleagues said we were crazy. "Who do you think you are?" they exclaimed, claiming that carrying a mobile phone was not something that normal people did. This made us the main laughingstock for some time (of course, today it's completely the other way around!).

Into The Wild In A Van Filled With Books

So, we stuffed a large van with books and started our journey. Our aim, like always in those kind of trips, was to return home with an empty van. The air was full of juvenile excitement, our journey started well and at our first stop, Höfn in Hornafjörður, we started selling. Höfn is a small town on the southeast corner of Iceland, so to arrive there we had to drive around the entire south coast with all its scenery like Jökulsárlón, our magnificent glacier lagoon, full of ice that comes from Vatnajökull, the largest glacier in Europe. Höfn's uniqueness is its proximity to the glacier. No other town is as dominated by Vatnajökull and nowhere else have people learned to live in such close quarters with a huge sheet of ice.

The weather in Höfn that day was typical Icelandic weather: Ever changing, snowy, and unpredictable. In Iceland, the weather is a constant issue of discussion, since it affects us so directly. In Iceland, you can always expect a bit of snow, a chance of rain, sunny streaks and windy moments – all within the same hour! We have a saying, especially for confused tourists: "If you don't like the weather, just wait fifteen minutes." Therefore, the issue of weather is a kind of a national sport and has often proven to be an effective icebreaker in awkward social situations.

This might be the reason why Icelanders are notoriously good at adapting to every situation … and likewise why we have trouble dealing with long–term planning, and why we tend to walk at a really fast pace. The weather is a huge factor of the everyday Icelandic lifestyle. We have to listen to it and sometimes we have to outrun it! For me, this can always translate into my area of expertise, sales and business. In my field, you constantly have to be able to read the current conditions and to predict the immediate future as accurately as possible.

Surrounded By Steep Cliffs In A Wild Storm

Saleswise we did OK in Höfn, but the car was still fully loaded with books. Djúpivogur was our next stop, an even smaller town northeast of Höfn, quite a distance, especially in those weather conditions. It was nonetheless an experience to drive through the dramatic landscapes of the east coast. Part of the way between Höfn and Djúpivogur one drives directly under a steep mountain on the left hand side and on your right side there are sharp cliffs which lead directly down to the turbulent Atlantic Ocean.

This part of the road, called 'the washboards', was notorious. During the summers, mud slides and falling rocks were frequent, and during the winter avalanches were always expected. This we knew, but still we didn't know what we had coming.

My colleague Óli was luckily a very experienced driver and I had driven many times through the perilous conditions of the West Fjords of Iceland, another territory where the roads are dangerous and the weather tends to be dramatic. When we were approaching the washboards, the storm had already increased and the snow was so heavy that we could barely see through the windows. Our hearts were already pounding harder. What had we gotten ourselves into? We had the mountain to our left and the steep cliffs and the sea to our right. The road was icy, and we crawled forward at a low speed, the car barely moving. Slowly, we were starting to realize the severity of the situation.

After some time, we had completely lost track of our location and how far we had driven. It didn't matter at all that this was supposed to be a familiar territory. The visibility diminished increasingly and we were starting to panic. Our only assistance was the yellow road sticks on the side of the road, since their diagonal reflective stickers would always point towards the road, instead of leading us into the sea. For a very long time we relied solely on these sticks for guidance.

Chances Of Disaster: Increasing

Since he wasn't driving, Sigurður kept an eye on the mountainside to our left. Out of nowhere, he said, almost to himself:

"This doesn't look good, an avalanche might hit us."

We didn't find this remark amusing, but Óli agreed, saying that exactly this particular area was one of the worst.

"It might as well happen right now," he said.

And then our worst fears began to materialize. We saw what seemed to be a slight movement in the snow on the mountain side before us, but we weren't sure so we kept crawling forward on our large and fully loaded van, meter by meter along the mountain road, hoping, simply hoping for the best.

All of a sudden a huge avalanche hit the road directly in front of us! We couldn't see a thing. Everything was totally white and we had no idea what would happen next. Everything was shaking and Óli stopped the car abruptly. In my memory, this chain of events is stored in super-slow-motion. Am I going to die, right here and now? Am I going to die here in the middle of nowhere, right now, in a van full of books? These were the thoughts racing through my head, out of control, and only moments after the avalanche had hit the road I thought: "Could there be another one coming?"

We didn't realize how close to us the avalanche had hit until we saw it slide down the mountainside, over the road and crash into the waves of the sea right in front of us. It had missed the car by just a few meters. We were lucky to be alive. The shock seeped in and, being paralyzed by the initial shock, we had no idea what to do. Was there another one coming? We had no idea. We just knew that if the first one had hit the car we would have crashed into the sea, and that we had no control and it could just as easily have hit our car. Could we turn the car around in these conditions? What should we do?

Another Avalanche?

All of us tried to think fast and we were feebly discussing some solutions to the situation. We couldn't leave the car and try to walk away, that would pose a huge risk. And the narrow road offered no space for a getaway. We were stuck between an avalanche and a hard place.

And then, all of a sudden, we heard the heavy and forceful rumbling of an avalanche! Another one was rushing down the mountainside. Would it hit us? For a split second we had no idea where it would hit. In front of us? Behind us? Would it hit the car and throw us into the ocean?

When the noise died out we looked at each other in amazement. *What had happened?*, we wondered. And then, we took a look.

The situation in front of the car was unchanged. The snow

from the first avalanche was still there, blocking our way forward.

The car was still on the road. We hadn't been hit.

We finally looked behind the van, and there we saw, to our amazement, that another avalanche had hit the road behind us! Only a couple of meters away from the van. We looked at each other, not believing our own eyes.

We are stuck between two avalanches!

After the first rush of panic, and after we had fully realized our luck, our only option was to use the super-expensive mobile phone that we had purchased for the trip – the one that had given so many people reason to make fun of us. We still had no idea if there was any kind of phone signal in that location, but when Óli tried to call the Search and Rescue Team in Höfn, I remember thinking: *How fortunate that we didn't allow the opinion of other people to control our actions!*

In retrospect, it was a classic life scenario. We had followed our instincts when buying the phone, tolerating the laughs and the nasty comments, but afterwards? Of course everyone considered the phone our best investment by far!

Rescue Is Coming, On A Snow Plough!

The Search and Rescue Team in Höfn said they had just one option: To send a snow plough our way. It could take hours in that crazy weather and we had no option but to wait in the cold and the snow. This was not a great option, since the heater in the van didn't work well. So, we started to figure out all kinds of ways to make the stay more bearable. Someone pointed out that heat always streams upwards, so we used all the books to mount ourselves higher in the van, sitting on top of stacks of books!

Shortly after our wait had begun, a red light appeared slowly in front of our van. We had no idea what was happening. *What or who was approaching?*

It was a Lada Sport, a small Russian jeep, approaching out of nowhere! How was this possible? We had seen the avalanche fall in front of us, but we had never seen this jeep!

We went out and fought through the snow and found a family of four! The couple was relieved to know that we had managed to get hold of the Search and Rescue Team. When I think about how relative our perspective in life can get, I always think about that couple and how calm they managed to stay despite the horrible circumstances of being trapped with their kids between two avalanches. It seems to be a universal truth: The important thing isn't what happens to us, only how we react to the things that happen to us. In all likelihood, they were also remaining composed in order to protect their kids, not wanting to frighten them by their own fear.

After a short chat we returned to our van, hoping that our wait wouldn't drag out for too long. And to our surprise, Óli pulled a large bottle of whiskey out of his duffel bag. To be honest, this is by far the best whiskey I have ever tasted, and back then I barely even liked whiskey! Just a few sips of it made us feel warm, and also quite intoxicated, very quickly! Somehow everything was feeling better, the cavalry was on its way and we tried to make the wait as comfortable as possible, despite the fact that another avalanche was always imminent.

After a long time the Search and Rescue Team showed up on a gigantic snow plough and they decided that the only possible solution was to leave the cars behind. The snow simply was too heavy and wet and the cars would have to be picked up the next day. We stepped inside the snowplough along with the family and literally drove over the avalanche and then all the way to Djúpivogur. Of course this was not the fastest vehicle around, but for some glorious reason the time went by quickly.

True Joy And The Feast Of A Lifetime

Maybe it was the whiskey? Because when we arrived, the bottle was empty and we were extremely light-headed. We were accompanied to a small and friendly guesthouse and the owners announced that we were free to eat and drink anything we would like. *Everything for the survivors!* Anything from the fridge, the freezers, the kitchen, and the bar. Everything was open for us and it was the grandest gesture of hospitality that I have ever experienced. The family soon went to sleep, but the rest of us, the young and spirited salespeople who had endured the experience, we ate and drank to our heart's delight! It was a magnificent evening and our relief was immense, especially when we realized, late at night, that we had luckily escaped death. Narrowly.

It was a totally exhausted bunch that dragged their feet to bed after a short party.

When we woke up the following day we were told that the road was being cleared. The weather had turned calm and sunny, and our van had not been thrown into the ocean. So, we had a few hours to kill before we could pick it up. We found a gas station with a diner and started playing cards after we finished our late lunch. The game was poker, playing for quarters. The stakes were low, but that didn't spoil a thing. As in business, it's fun playing, no matter if the odds are low or high.

Óli was winning, but suddenly I realized that he was cheating. And to put it mildly, I didn't take this well. Óli just started laughing:

"Come on! You know I never cheat. I'm just messing with you."

"I don't care if we are playing for quarters," I replied. "You know how I feel about cheating and dishonesty."

Óli wouldn't back down and frankly enjoyed himself.

"This is not the way to play," I added. I took the few coins I had left off the table and walked over to the counter. The young waitress, having witnessed the whole scenario, looked a bit startled when I came over and said to her:

"You know, since I've lost almost all my coins through the dishonesty of my friend, I'm going to spend the rest on a scratchcard ticket."

She looked at me like I was a pillaging Viking, sword raised and ready for battle.

"You wanna pick one?" she asked with a trembling voice, handing over a large stack of tickets.

I told her that I really didn't care and then I took one random ticket from the stack, went over to Óli and said:

"How about you lend me a quarter so I can scratch this ticket?"

Óli was amused by all of this and handed me a coin, but his face changed quickly when I started scratching. The ticket said:

Europe – Europe – Europe.

I had won a trip to Europe!

More Luck And A Trip To Europe

Not only was I lucky to be alive, I had won a trip to Europe that would eventually take me to Copenhagen and Kiel, Germany. Everything had changed in an instant. I went from crazy mad to crazy happy, screaming with joy. Óli's cheating had been a blessing in disguise and I walked over to him and said:

"This is what cheating me gets you!"

His response? A short time later, after we had left the diner, he went back in and bought the rest of the tickets. He bought all of them for thousands of Icelandic krona. And what did he get?

Absolutely nothing at all.

To make a long story short, we returned to our van a bit later, thrilled to be alive and to be able to continue on our adventurous sales trip.

We had not survived an avalanche, we had survived two of them!

Thrown Off My Feet, Literally!

So, maybe the lesson we learned was that during the high winter, Reykjavík was a better place to explore. Reykjavík, however, also had its perilous moments. One incident will never ever leave me. One night I was selling at a large apartment building. I knocked on a door on the 5th floor but no one answered. I waited for a while and then I knocked again.

All of a sudden the door ripped open and a tall, slim guy came out. He was furious, asking what the hell I was doing there. He shouted at me that all sales were forbidden in the building and told me to f**k off and get out. After this, everything happened really fast. He pushed me backwards so I fell towards the nearby elevator and pushed the button so it opened instantly. He shoved me into the elevator and I tumbled down, books and price lists spreading all over the floor. He stood angrily in front of me, arms crossed and legs spread, and pressed the button to send the elevator to the ground floor. The door closed, the guy disappeared and I descended, in total shock.

I didn't realize what had happened until I reached the ground floor. Without serious thought, I composed myself, gathered my books and price lists, took the elevator back up again, intending to confront the guy. Echoing in my mind were the words of Guðmundur, my former sales manager:

*"The moment you lose your self-respect, you should pack up and leave
the sales business!"*

I knocked on the door and the guy opened. His face was terrified when he saw how angry I was, and I was furious! I poked
his shoulder firmly and pushed him into the apartment. Before
I knew it we had ended up in his living room. Trying to make
up for the height difference – I didn't want to look up at him – I
ordered him to sit down. And he complied.

Then I gave him my full speech:

"In the future you are going to show people who are simply
trying to do their jobs your respect! That's the only thing I'm
doing here, this is my job! You could have easily showed me
some basic respect without having to buy books from me. Not
to mention throwing me into the elevator!"

During these few seconds, his whole demeanor changed
drastically. He went from rage to fear and from there he went
into tears, crying in front of me and saying:

"I'm sorry, I'm sorry. It's just that …when you initially
knocked on my door, I had just been told about a death in the
family."

I was blown away. At first I couldn't say anything, and the
shift in my attitude was full and complete. I felt the rage slip
rapidly away and it was replaced by shame. I told him how
sorry I was, and that I had no way of knowing this. He told me
not to worry and then we embraced each other and he bought a
bunch of books from me. No, that's actually not true (although I
have, on a rare occasion, told this fairytale version of the story).
But he did tell me not to worry and we left the crazy scenario
having fully made up, with no grudges. We parted as friends
and I sincerely felt that this was just a decent guy having a very
lousy day.

All this happened in just a few moments, but the memory

will last a lifetime. This made me realize, fully and deeply, that we can never really know what goes on inside other people and in their lives. This was also the last time I allowed someone to offend me, and my motto since this day has been:

– No one can offend you without your permission.

Of course it's always a question of what perspective you have towards yourself and others, no matter if you are fighting an inner or outer struggle, with other people, yourself, or with nature.

The Big Lesson

Being a traveling salesman in Iceland during these times was no picnic, especially since both the vehicles and the roads were much worse than they are today.

One Saturday, a few of us book salesmen took off on a sales trip together. The weather was beautiful, the sky was still clear, but there was a prospect of rain. We hadn't driven for long when the rain started pouring down, and then the wind started blowing and the weather escalated very quickly into a full-blown rainstorm.

We stopped at a small diner in the middle of nowhere, had some traditional sugary pancakes and coffee and discussed how we would proceed. Most of them wanted to return, but I, soaking wet, wouldn't hear of it. We could barely walk between houses, but I stubbornly insisted that we should continue selling, thinking that the weather may even strengthen our chances, since people would invite us inside. Engilbert was our team-leader and after some discussion I managed to convince him. He had the deciding vote, so we decided to carry on.

Our destination was the small town of Hveragerði – the hot

springs capital of the world. It's a magical but humble town. Throughout the year you can see the steam rising from numerous geysers in the town. During summer the town is a green community, abounding with beautiful trees, and full of large greenhouses where all year round you can grow your own vegetables, exclusively using the heat from the ground.

We arrived around noon and Engilbert split us up into two separate neighborhoods. We were to walk between houses all day, meet up for dinner and check our statuses and decide how long we would stay in Hveragerði.

At dinner, I found out that everyone had sold something … except me. I hadn't sold a single book. My colleagues however were quite happy with the results of their day's work.

We decided to continue through the evening. I walked and I walked from door to door, but no one wanted to buy anything from me, no one had the slightest interest. I kept getting NO, NO, NO.

Using Humor To Break The Ice

How did I keep myself going? I used a way of thinking that has helped me on countless occasions. It goes like this:

To get one YES I will go through a lot of NOs. They are, in fact, an integral part of each YES. If I divide my earnings with the number of NOs, I will actually figure out how much I am getting paid for each NO, turning them into a positive element of the sales process.

This tough day, I received some pretty strange remarks and negative comments. People were using all the excuses in the book not to say yes to what I was offering. Some said they already had all the books in my catalogue, which was highly unlikely. I remember that on this particular day I often used a lame joke of mine:

Potential client: "No thanks. I already have all these books."

Me: "But how about the fourteen volume epic publication of *Gunnar Andri's Life and Travel?*"

Potential client (with a hint of a smile): "Sure, I own that one too."

Me: "Well, that's fantastic, because I just recently published *Gunnar Andri's Life and Travel? Vol. II.* You must be interested in buying that one, being a fan?"

Admittedly, this approach is just a joke and it might be a bit cheesy, but if you can get people to laugh or smile, you can get them to buy. However, don't try this if humor is not in your nature. Only do it if it comes naturally. During these days I hadn't studied the art of sales like I have done today, but I managed to sell by being myself, by being honest.

In my opinon, before people can buy a product or a service from you, they first have to buy into the concept of you as a fellow human being! They have to like you to a certain extent and they also have to feel some kind of trust and bond.

The Very Last Sale Can Change Everything

But this wasn't happening for me on this particular day in Hveragerði. Time passed on, I kept on doing my rounds between houses in the cold evening darkness. As a rule, we didn't knock on doors after 10 pm. I only had five minutes left, and still I hadn't sold a single copy. I had a few houses to go and decided to finish them all, thinking about how the opera isn't over, and how quitting can easily turn into a bad habit. Winners never quit – quitters never win. This became my mantra.

And then I knocked on the last door. A man and his wife answered, and the first thing I saw was ...bookshelves! In my experience, people with bookshelves tend to like books, even love them. Clearly I had entered a book-loving home and I could also see right away that these people had money, since they had quality books all around.

So, I pulled out my big guns, presenting all the finest books and collections I had with me. And after this long and hard day, I ended up making a single sale of a total of 50 books, including the entire collector's edition of Halldór Laxness, our most important and renowned author, who received the Nobel Prize in Literature in 1955. The couple told me that they were buying some of these books for the second time, having already given books to their children from their private collection. They stressed the importance of reading and emphasized that all children should be presented with quality literature. I couldn't agree more, since 'readers are leaders and leaders are readers'. Through the years, I have learned to never lend my books to friends or family. I would rather lend people money than my books. My books are full of scribbles and underlining that are extremely valuable to me.

At the end of the day, my colleagues and I met up to compare our performances. The total sales numbers were great, and everyone was happy we didn't return home earlier. And what do you know? My single sale put me on top of the group! To this day I have tried to remember to always keep going, keep going, keep going. And, that you get paid for hearing this wonderful word:

NO!

The Last Book Sales Run

My most vivid memory from my book selling period, however, is from my very last sales run. At the time I had just met my daughter's mother. She was blond, tall, extremely smart, and I had a major crush on her. Despite being only 19 years old, she already spoke many languages, including Greek, after having lived in Greece with her family for some time.

This ability offered her the fantastic opportunity to work as a tour guide in Cyprus, guiding Icelandic groups to Israel and Egypt for three and a half months. I encouraged her to go, and promised that I would join her two weeks after she had arrived, as soon as I had earned enough money to be able to afford the trip. My goal was to earn enough money to be able to spend three months with her, carefree and happy. Of course she asked me if this was a realistic goal. To live in Cyprus for a whole three months without working, having enough money for food and drink and accommodations?

I will never forget the moment that I promised her that I would achieve this goal. I didn't have much time, so I had to begin right away. A month was all the time I had.

This time I didn't go on a sales trip with other salesmen. I simply went from door to door by myself, and I also decided to isolate myself completely during this important project. I notified my friends, told them about my project and asked for their understanding, letting them know that I wouldn't be attending any parties or events. The only thing I did was sell books and more books.

To reach my goal I knew I had to sell very well the whole time. That's why I put my main emphasis on the large book collections we had in stock, instead of the lighter novels that were easier to sell.

I was selling each night and my girlfriend didn't have a land line in Greece. To make things easier we decided that she would call me on a particular day at a particular time, and if I didn't answer she was to pick me up at the airport because that would mean I was on my way to meet her.

From Hell To Paradise

It was pure hell, apart from the fact of how excited I was about the end results of the project. During the final evenings of my manic sales run, I had abused my energy to the point that I was throwing up when I came home at night. I was completely exhausted, both mentally and physically; I had used up all my strength and energy, and felt over-worked and exhausted.

Therefore, my victory was super sweet. I had earned everything myself, all this luxury I was about to experience.

I went to Cyprus, greeted my girlfriend at the airport and simply had the time of my life. Everything was worth it, despite the sacrifices I had to make. Living in Cyprus for three months with no worries, no TV, no phone, no sales, without any fuss or frenzy. It was pure paradise.

It was a very relaxing period for me, even though at this time Iceland was still very quiet and low–key. For example, up until 1983 our only state–run TV station in Iceland was closed during the month of July, so we could enjoy the summer even more. And up until 1987 this same station didn't broadcast anything on Thursdays, so that families could share quality moments at least once a week.

Of course at that time, I had no idea the importance of being at peace with yourself. It's only now, years later, that I fully understand this. If you have the chance to travel and broaden your horizons, by all means, do it! Collecting memories is far more important than collecting stuff.

So, my time in Cyprus was hard-earned but fantastic. My girlfriend and I had a great time together, taking numerous day trips to both Israel and Egypt. We became engaged in Bethlehem and our rings were blessed by a Greek Orthodox priest.

The engagement was supposed to be our little secret, but my girlfriend was a tour guide on a huge ocean liner and one of the passengers noticed the ring and let everyone else know. Before we knew it, everyone on board was celebrating and congratulating us. Over 700 passengers sharing our happiness and joy!

This magnificent period in my life was priceless, and it would never have been possible but for the fact that I worked unfailingly towards my goal. I went ALL IN!

For me, that is the only way possible: You don't do things in a mediocre way, you have to go ALL IN, you have to DO instead of TRY, because like the saying goes:

Trying is lying!

In the end, everything will turn out in one way or another, although many people may doubt this fact along the way.

Halldór Laxness – Independent People

Messages From The Middle Of Nowhere

– Keep your honesty intact, it will return to you many times over.

– Our life situation really doesn't matter, it's how we respond to it that does.

– There is a fundamental difference between a pricey object and an expensive one.

– Treat everyone with respect. Everyone, always!

– You can become the best at skills you are worst at.

– Experiencing new cultures will help you discover new sides of yourself.

– No one can offend you without your permission.

– If you can get people to laugh or smile, you can get them to buy.

– Before people can buy a product or a service from you, they first have to buy into the concept of you.

– Collecting memories is far more important than collecting stuff.

– You have to go ALL IN, you have to DO instead of TRY, because Trying is lying!

And last but not least:

– Don't allow the opinion of other people to control your actions!

CHAPTER 5

Erupt From Within
And Nothing Will Stop You

From Books To Home Appliances

Hafnarfjörður is a port town and municipality located on the southwest coast of Iceland, about 10 km south of Reykjavík. Each year, Hafnarfjörður hosts an annual Viking festival where Viking culture enthusiasts from around the world display reconstructions of Viking handicraft and put on sword-fighting shows.

My search for fortune and happiness one day led me to Hafnarfjörður as I went there for a job interview. The job in question was later to make an entrepreneur of me, abroad. The company was selling vacuum cleaners through pre-booked visits to peoples homes. I would be lying if I said I was initially excited about this job, but what interested me was the opportunity involved.

The premise was this: You could climb the ladder within the company, and in Iceland that was a rare opportunity in those days. This was my prime reason for jumping aboard. They also had a very convincing seminar and study course. It was usually done in four days, but since I had experience and they were impressed with my interview, they decided to allow me to conclude it in a day and a half.

I decided that even though I already knew I was a good salesman, I would be broad-minded about this study course. opening up to any kind of guidance. My greatest take-away was this: *It takes four years to become a chef, but you still haven't become a master chef.* Still, many people seem to think they have learned everything about salesmanship after just four days.

Mastery Takes Time

I have used this philosophy in my own courses for about 20 years. It's very common that people expect to be taught everything in a few hours. But those that manage to acquire skills in this business know that the key to success is returning again and again, even to the same seminars. It's the same with showering: it isn't enough to take a single shower. Ask anyone who has tried it.

The best of the best see themselves as perpetual students, always seeking more knowledge and finding out new ways to remind themselves about the things that they already know. It's a matter of always staying alert and ready, keeping your swords and knives prepared before the battle begins.

When I started selling for Kirby, there was an ongoing sales competition that had started three months earlier. The winner would receive flight tickets to Denmark and Paris with a full package of accomodations and meals for the duration of the trip. When I entered the competition there were only three weeks left, so I had to step up my game in order to have a chance at winning.

My experience was good and the decision to be broad-minded paid off. I did really well, my income was fantastic, I scored some bonuses, and in the end, yes, I won both of the trips for my girlfriend and me.

From Envy To Enlightenment

But that's not the main point here. What amazed me was that almost all the other salesmen were preoccupied with trying to calculate how much I had managed to earn. Only one of them approached me, congratulated me and even asked if he could watch and learn from me. I would have been happy to help anyone who had asked me, but he was the only one.

This guy had really fought for his success. I admired his resilience and how he never gave up. Shortly after this I took him under my wing and his results started improving almost instantly. This for me was proof that in sales you have to obey certain laws, just like in any other field.

I always try to remember that we can never shy away from asking for assistance or help. As a general rule, successful people are more than willing to share their own experience. The key lies in simply asking. The worst-case scenario? Someone says no to you. And life goes on, leaving you in the same position as before. Universally, the same things block us from success. It's the fear of failure and the fear of rejection. Or, to put it another way:

The fear of NO!

A Born Salesman?

Our sales meetings were held once a week, and one day a supplier remarked:

"Well, Gunnar Andri, of course, is a born salesman."

I interrupted him and strongly objected to his theory. I told him that I was not at all a born salesman and then I explained how I had, amongst numerous other books, rigorously studied *How To Master The Art Of Selling* by Tom Hopkins and taken it with me on numerous sales trips in Iceland. That particular book is underlined, scribbled in and highlighted all over its pages, with different pens, pencils and colors. For me, this is the only proper way of reading a book you really want to grasp. The first time, using a pencil for underlining, marking everything that tickles your attention, something of value or special interest. Then, for the second round, I find it very useful to highlight those extra juicy bits that you know you must remember permanently. A point to add in this context is that it's better to read a single book and abide by its principles than to read numerous books and fail to grasp their content!

Even after I had given this small speech on the literature that had turned me into a good salesman, people were still saying that this was a load of rubbish, that either you are born a salesman or you're not. Someone added that guiding people without this 'gift' was almost impossible. I experienced the whole thing like a sort of a joke, but maybe the joke was on me and other salesmen that were selling almost as much as me? Maybe people just took me for a buffoon? This whole experience got under my skin and stayed with me for some years, because my belief, probably borrowed along the way from my friend Brian Tracy, is that 'all skills are learnable'.

The Art Of Small Talk

If quality salespeople have one trait in common, it's that they have good abilities in human interaction. And a large part of my approach, ever since my book-selling years, is the belief that conversing with strangers is by far the best way to practice the skill of human interaction. If you can easily start a conversation with a complete stranger, then you have already acquired one of the most important traits there are.

Ironically, this course of events led me to dig deep into the field of personal development. I didn't understand the resistance of my fellow salesmen and I firmly believed in this approach. I still do. I believe that your sales won't improve until you yourself have become a more amiable person.

The Brian Tracy Revolution

The American mother company sent us six cassettes with a Brian Tracy seminar called *Set Your Sights On Success*. I fell in love with this approach, to put it mildly. The tapes were 60 minutes each and I listened to all of them, three times in a row. That's 18 hours straight!

I will never forget how impressed I was. I asked all the flight attendants I knew (plus everyone I knew who was traveling abroad) to bring back books and tapes about sales and marketing, especially this emerging field of 'personal development'. I studied hard, all the time, even changing my car into a traveling university, never listening to radio stations but focusing instead on the likes of Brian Tracy, Zig Ziglar, Jim Ron, and Tony Robbins.

I even used this method to learn Greek. My girlfriend at this time had lived in Greece and we created our own linguaphone for Icelandic/Greek. She would record particular sentences that I would listen to repeatedly and try to pronounce, over and over again. Later on, when I lived in Greece for a period, these lessons were to come in really handy.

For me, this method is as relevant today as before. Even if technology has advanced (and audio cassettes are now outdated), all the same principles apply. You can use all the time you spend on the road for self-education and empowerment. The same applies when working out or going for a run, You always have a choice between 'shallow' entertainment, music, radio stations, or your own education. The Internet is swarming with good stuff about almost any subject you can imagine. Some if it is totally free of charge, other options cost a few dollars, such as books, seminars, lectures, and insights. This way, you can stay forever current with your approach

You wouldn't trust a doctor that hasn't updated his methods since graduation, would you?

Education Versus Entertainment

Some years ago, I stumbled upon a very interesting concept called EvE (no, I'm not referring to EVE Online, the fantastic Icelandic computer game). I am referring to the EvE Ratio: Education vs. Entertainment. According to this ratio, 1 out of 100 people spends 100 hours in fun or entertainment for each 1 hour spent on personal development, knowledge building or self-education.

I'm sure that in some groups, these numbers are even worse. Every single person I know who has achieved something great, be it in sports, business or another field of life, is constantly working towards keeping in shape and adding to the skills and knowledge. I'm pretty sure that the same applies to the achievers you know personally.

The average person spends 100 times more time and money

in some sort of entertainment (TV, coffee houses, social media, movies, theater) than on personal development (taking courses or seminars, reading books). This equals disaster, in my view, because if you're not getting better you're getting worse. Life is in continuous motion, and status quo simply doesn't exist. We live in a world that is filled with people who claim they want a career or something better but do nothing about it. Part of the reason may be their lack of thirst for knowledge, and knowledge is an essential part of personal development because it can never be taken away from you.

On The Road With A Pregnant Girlfriend

When my girlfriend was six months pregnant, we decided to take a sales trip together to North–Iceland. Our ride was an old Mazda 323 and we called it Guðmundur (a common Icelandic name, just 'Ask Guðmundur'!) because it definitely was a car with an old soul. Its only purpose was getting us from A to B, so we filled Guðmundur up with vacuum cleaners and started our trip.

Our first stop was Skagaströnd, a small coastal town. We had our first presentation that same night and it was a huge success, as we sold several items. It was a fun night, which was important, since positive vibes always lead to more sales.

Skagaströnd turned out to be a very beautiful and cozy town, so we, being young and free and full of spirit, decided to stay there for a couple of nights in a tent we had taken along with us. These few nights turned into a whole month. We set up a base there, breathing in the fresh country air and enjoying the unique arctic Icelandic summer. A month in a tent turned out to be an unforgettable experience. The skies were bright all night long, one of the benefits of Icelandic summers, since we have extensive darkness during the winters instead.

It was high summer. We lived in a tent and used a primus to cook our humble meals. We went to the swimming pool to refresh ourselves and take a shower. Once a week we drove to Reykjavík to get our clothes washed and to run some errands. Thinking about these times and how we solved our situation with simplicity, I sometimes wonder about all the excuses we are able to come up with today for not achieving success.

Because of this good spirit, our trip turned into pure success and sales skyrocketed. This market area was promising to begin with, filled with rather wealthy families from one of our main industries, the fishing industry. But the main reason for the success was that we managed to establish trust. My girlfriend was pregnant and both of us approached this mission with honesty and sincerity. And when you have trust, all decision-making is simpler. When you generally lack trust, like when we experienced the economic crash in Iceland in 2008, business becomes hard and stifled. The internal life and state of the salesman will always reach the customer to some extent. To sum up: If you feel great, you will do great.

Selling ... Against All Odds

When this wave of selling vacuum cleaners was at its peak, we had over 60 salesmen on the job. Considering that the total population of Iceland was then around 300,000 inhabitants, this was a whole lot. The company had been successful, many individual salesmen had been extremely successful, and some of them considered this area to be fully exploited. A competing brand had entered the market with force, and closing a sale had become increasingly difficult in this limited market on an isolated island in the middle of nowhere.

So, the mood had gone. Our best salesmen found numerous excuses for their lack of sales, blaming everything and nothing, and also received some bad coverage in the press. They claimed that people were no longer willing to recommend the product to their friends and family, making it hard to find proper prospects.

In my mind, making excuses is a slippery slope, especially for salesmen. We are experts in the art of convincing, so if we find a convincing excuse, we readily convince ourselves that it is the truth! And so, we get stuck and can't move on. Everything you focus on will grow, just like when you consider buying a particular car, then start seeing that car everywhere!

This mini–empire therefore seemed to be crumbling. Salesmen started deserting, convinced that they couldn't live on their percentages from sales only. In the end, they all gave up. So did the supplier and the importer, they all quit. Except one salesman.

Yes, you guessed it.

Me.

I continued. And this time around, I had another mission, even though most people told me I was crazy to even think I would sell some more.

But my plan and incentive was this: I was going to move to Greece and therefore my goal was to sell 52 vacuum cleaners in a limited amount of time!

To make it more real, I created a visual aid. I bought a deck of cards and for each sale I wrote on it the name of the customer and removed it from the deck. These served as private incentives, because no one knew about this self–competition but me. And the deck of cards? I still have it and keep it along my most prized possessions: my diaries.

Having Goals And Sticking To Them

I could write a whole book about setting goals and how to achieve them to become successful. But for now, I will stick to a few essentials before I continue with the story.

First, you have to have a **burning passion** for the goal to become a reality. And when I say a burning passion, I mean in the sense that you imagine having more force than Mount Hekla, one of Iceland's most active volcanoes with over 20 eruptions since 874, nicknamed 'Gateway to Hell' by Europeans in the Middle Ages. If you have true passion and you start to erupt, then nothing will stop you from exploding.

Second, you need to convince yourself that you **really can** reach your goal. This is what I refer to as The Fight Between Fire and Ice. Fire is your inner force and conviction, but Ice is your self-doubt and restraints. This conflict is characterized both in the Icelandic psyche and the Icelandic landscape. Our largest glacier (and also Europe's largest) has a surface area of 8,100 km2. Generally measuring 400–600 meters in thickness and reaching 950 meters in height, the glacial ice conceals a number of mountains, valleys and plateaus. It even hides some active central volcanoes, of which Bárðarbunga is the largest and Grímsvötn the most active.

Third but not last, you need to write your goal down, after you have succeeded in the fight between Fire and Ice. And the best way to create an extra incentive is to promise someone close to you that you are going to reach the goal. This leads to a resilient mindset, focusing on solutions rather than excuses.

Adding to the incentive, you can also straight-out promise someone close to you some direct benefits, if you succeed your goal. I have frequently used this motivation through the years and it has worked every single time. If you have a family, this can also create an additional support for your project and goal, so when the work hours are long you get your family's full support instead of grunting and disappointment.

The Reasons Behind Failed Goals

Dealing with goals, it's very important to realize exactly why people fail to achieve them. One important element is writing the goal down, even doing so repeatedly, and reading the goal aloud, over and over again. Our hearts and minds seem to acknowledge this kind of 'chanting' and it makes our efforts even stronger.

Another part of this discussion depends on whether you reach all your goals or not. It is actually OK if you don't reach the goal. It's not the end of the world and it's not an indication that you should quit. Setting the goal is a huge victory, sharpening your focus with the goal is another victory, reaching a larger portion of your goal than you are used to, it all matters. Setting a goal sets your general direction and fills you with power, transporting you further than you would have gone without the goal.

I told my former colleagues what my goal was in selling the American vacuum cleaners and that my aim was to move to Greece and settle there. They replied with scorn, telling me it was hopeless, saying that the times had changed. I remember one girl saying to me:

"If you sell 15 units in one month, I'll buy you a bottle of Champagne."

Most of them were acting out of kindness, giving me tips and warning me away from trying in certain places and towns like Neskaupsstaður, Siglufjörður, Skagafjörður, Svarfaðardalur and certain neighborhoods in Reykjavík.

What was my stubborn reaction to this? I made a list out of their 'hopeless' places and went directly there. To cut a long story short, I reached my goal of 52 sales easily! And I did it in rural areas that were deemed impossible because other salesmen had already tried selling on every farm and in every home. During times when previous sales of 15 units had been the norm but selling 4 units had now become a decent monthly outcome, I was able to sell 14 units in one week.

How did I do this? How was this possible?

To be honest, it really wasn't complicated. I followed the three principles above in a rigorous manner, writing the goals down and repeating my mantras about them. My attitude towards the project was this: It's not a matter of IF I'm going to reach the goal, the only question is HOW.

What You Want And Why You Want It

The message in all of this is clear: Figure out what you want and WHY you want it. The way to reach your goal will dawn on you, eventually, if your first premise is clear. You will draw towards yourself everything that is needed for the fulfillment of the goal, even from unexpected directions.

My motive for reaching my goal was really strong, although I didn't know exactly how to get there. Your WHY has by far the strongest impact on your success. The stronger your reason is, and the more strength you have for the battle itself, the easier it becomes for you to think in solutions rather than problems, already visualizing the final victory. Echoing the words of Napoleon Hill in his book *Think and Grow Rich*:

"Whatever the mind can see and believe, the mind can achieve."

So, during this mad sales run of mine, I carried my written goals with me, wherever I went, reading them again and again whenever I had a chance. It was a constant visualization, and right now, writing this book, I am visualizing hordes of avid readers, reading the book I am writing. If you have tried this method I am sure you can confirm that it works. If you have not, then I would encourage you to write down your goals, carry them with you at all times, read them again and again, and visualize yourself achieving the goals you set.

Don't Fix On Long-Term Goals

There is no need to think in long-term goals. It's more efficient to break them down to goals for the month, the week, the day, even for specified hours of the day. Doing this will help you believe that reaching the long-term goal is, indeed, possible.

Remember: If the forces deep within you are willing to fight, you have already won the war before entering the battle.

What also kept me going was the way I started looking at the project itself. I knew the approximate statistics between the numbers of people at each presentation versus number of sales. This lead me to focus solely on the number of people getting exposed to my sales approach, instead of focusing on how much I planned to sell on a particular day. Instead of focusing on making sales calls, trying to dig up prospects and possible leads, I did something that had never been done in Iceland before: I started selling vacuum cleaners door to door, knocking on one house after another, letting nothing get in my way.

One day, my car broke down in the middle of nowhere and my only solution was to hitchhike with all my stuff. People approaching in a car saw a peculiar stranded guy at the side of the road, and of course they had to stop to check what was going on. Seeing the notorious Icelandic sheep roaming free on the roads in Iceland is a common thing, but seeing a businessman with many bags and a huge vacuum cleaner in a box, that's quite remarkable.

Removing Obstacles

One of the strategies that made this sales run successful was that I decided to trade in older types of this particular vacuum cleaner in exchange for a brand new unit. After each sale I would send the used unit to my girlfriend in Reykjavík and she would place an ad in the newspapers and sell it. The funny thing about this arrangement was that people started saying, both to me and my girlfriend, that I would never reach my goal, since so many people were selling their used vacuum cleaners of this brand in the papers! I'm convinced that I was responsible for at least 90% of these ads at the time.

When it comes to numbers and figures, I'm pretty sure that people generally didn't realize that my salary was equal to that of a lawyer at the time. And I was selling household items! It's from this experience that one of my mottos was coined:

I'd rather be a top-notch vacuum cleaner salesman than a mediocre lawyer.

Imagine The Ultimate Success

"It doesn't matter what it is that you do – just aim to become the best in your business." Set an ambitious goal for yourself and work your way up to the top 5% if you aren't there already. At the top: that's where you'll find the real money, whatever your business is, because your own ambition is your best ruthless boss.

Does money buy happiness? Of course not. It's not the richest people that are the happiest. It's the ones that are growing, evolving, maturing, learning; the ones who are headed towards a particular goal. They are the ones that have reached the top. And of course money is relevant and important, too. But other things come first. Just ask any millionaire who has serious health issues. Would he trade in his wealth for better health? Of course, on any given day! Health is our ultimate goal, physical health but also mental and spiritual health, both individually and as a society.

We all long for health, longevity, and peace. We are almost constantly reminded of this here in Reykjavík, ever since Yoko Ono, influential artist and wife of the late John Lennon, had The Imagine Peace Tower built and launched in the city in 2007. The Tower is a beautiful tower of light, situated on the small island of Viðey, and it is lit during the darkest months of the Icelandic winter, attracting hordes of tourists and fans of Yoko and Lennon who want to encourage peace on a global scale. On the foundation of the tower, the words 'Imagine Peace' are carved in 24 different languages. It's really impressive and peaceful, and I am very fond of the fact that Yoko's original idea for this piece of art was conceived in 1967, the same year I was born.

Is this book about sales practices? Maybe, maybe not. Maybe it's about a way of life and having a new perspective. It really doesn't matter where we find ourselves in this world, deep inside we all want the same things. We want to experience happiness, maintain our health, and achieve financial freedom. For this reason, I usually get the same answer from wealthy individuals when I ask them to define success:

Success is fulfillment and inner peace.

That, in the end, is our ultimate goal, whatever our place in society.

Messages From The Middle Of Nowhere

– It doesn't matter where you are coming from, it only matters where you are going.

– The best of the best see themselves as perpetual students, always seeking more knowledge and finding out new ways to remind themselves about the things that they already know.

– It's better to read a single book and abide to its principle than to read numerous books and fail to grasp their content.

– Keep your swords and knives ready before the battle begins.

– Mediocrity is there for a reason.

– Everyone wants happiness, health, and financial freedom.

– It's not the richest people who are the happiest, it's the ones who are growing.

– Money is at the top, whatever your business is.

– It doesn't matter what it is that you do, just aim to become the best in your business.

– If you can easily start a conversation with a complete stranger, then you have already acquired one of the most important traits there are.

– Your sales won't improve until you yourself have become a more amiable person.

– Knowledge is an essential part of personal development because it can never be taken away from you.

– Don't focus on long-term goals. Break them down into months, weeks, days, and hours.

– Always be unstoppable!

– When you have trust, all decision-making is simpler.

– If you feel great, you will do great.

– Your own ambition is your best ruthless boss.

– We are experts in the art of convincing, so if we find a convincing excuse we have no problem convincing ourselves that it is the truth.

– Everything you focus on will grow.

– Figure out what you want and why you want it.

– If the forces deep within you are willing to fight, you have already won the war before entering the battle.

– If you haven't written your goal down, it will continue to be a dream.

– It's not a matter of IF you're going to reach the goal, the only question is HOW.

– Keep competing with yourself.

– Create an extra incentive by promising someone close to you that you are going to reach the goal.

– Your WHY has by far the strongest impact on your success. The stronger your reason, the more strength you have for the battle itself.

– Write down your goals, carry them with you at all times, and read them whenever possible.

– You need to convince yourself that you can reach your goal. This is what I refer to as The Fight Between Fire and Ice.

– If you feel great, you will do great.

– If you're not getting better, you're getting worse.

And last but not least:

– If you have true passion and you start to erupt, then nothing will stop you from exploding.

CHAPTER 6

Opening Doors From Greece And Back To Iceland

Dreams are like balloons: If you hold onto them and never let go, chances are that they will elevate you and carry you to your final destination. Equally true: If your grip isn't tight enough, in all likelihood your dreams and balloons will slip away, leaving you stranded in mid-air or even falling.

Dreaming Of Greece

Through the years I have had many dreams, some of them have materialized but others haven't; at least not yet. And once I had the dream of moving to Greece, that glorious country where the sun shines so brightly (ten times brighter than in Iceland, for sure). To be exact it was Thessaloniki, the second largest city in Greece, which my heart was set on.

I am a man of heat and sunshine, which is kind of complicated when you live in Iceland. Of course we get our fair share of beautiful summer days and I am always grateful for them, but the temperature never gets too high and, in some summers, sunny days are rare. On the other hand, there are other elements in Iceland that we take for granted that are in no way a common thing for most citizens of the world. Our clean water, for example. We have an abundance of clean water and we don't usually give it much thought when we allow it to flow freely from the tap or when we drink amounts of it, straight from the tap, straight from the source, clean and chemical–free.

Iceland is a small but dynamic country and thanks to the thermal energy and hydroelectric power, we have many options in renewable energy. This leads to low cost in heating and electricity for businesses and homes. We can still stay warm and cozy indoors, even if it is freezing outside. These advantages make me feel very grateful that I was born in Iceland. Even though our winters can be harsh with winds and snowstorms, they have their magical elements, too. One of these elements is our precious Aurora Borealis – The Northern Lights.

This mesmerizing dance of green, pink, and purple lights on the pitch-black sky has been a part of our natural habitat since the early settlement. There is nothing quite like standing in nature, surrounded by volcanoes, waterfalls and glaciers, watching this celestial show of the elements.

Of course, I tended to sometimes take this magic for granted. Isn't this often the case with the most precious elements in our own life? Where does your gratitude lie? What are you thankful for? The sooner you figure this out, the better. Choose to be grateful. It will bring you inner peace, tranquility, and happiness, all of which will come in handy in times of duress. And staying grateful for extended periods of time will lead to countless positive changes in your life.

True gratefulness will make you more connected to yourself and your inner life. You will experience more joy and love, and your eyes will be open to see all the opportunities around you. Just be ready to conquer the world – because your gratefulness for the smaller things in life will bring you more of the big stuff.

Trials And Obstacles In a Foreign Culture

So, back to my story about Greece and my 'imminent world domination'. My girlfriend and I had moved to the Greek city of Thessaloniki. And I soon got the feeling that I had lived there in another lifetime. I became 'Greek' overnight.

I had two main reasons for moving to Greece. First, my girlfriend spoke Greek and had lived there before. But the other reason was the hierarchy within the American vacuum cleaner company I had been selling for. In this company, it was possible to work yourself up to becoming a distributor, and I had achieved that with my mad sales run, having received the company's highest merit, the President's Award, the only salesman in Iceland to achieve that status.

I therefore moved to Greece filled with confidence and optimism, arriving in that warm and familiar country, set on making everything work out. Back in Iceland, I had sold all my belongings, creating a fresh start for the both of us.

Our first job in Greece was founding our company, SKALA Ltd., but that proved to be quite problematic. Very soon while in Greece I started getting the feeling that business wasn't always as proper as it should be.

We got into touch with a well-respected lawyer. During that time, he was all over the Greek media, working as a defender in a huge drug trafficking case, the largest one in 10 years. When we first met him, he found it impressive (and almost amusing, I think) to meet a young Icelandic couple that had traveled all the way to Greece to establish a vacuum cleaner company, where the salesman (me) spoke just the little bit of Greek he had learned from homemade linguaphone tapes!

This guy turned out to be just great and we soon became pretty close. I had to see him often and he was almost always busy when I arrived, dealing with clients. But Maria, his secretary, would always come running in very high heels, acting like a genuine Greek goddess, chanting "Andri, Andri, Andri!" (I used my second name in Greece for convenience and simplification). Then she would knock on his door and he would ask the person to step outside while he dealt with me.

Many of his clients looked dark and dubious, dressed in thick and heavy leather overcoats, bearded and rough. And I still remember the expression on their faces when I, the Icelander, walked in the room, always 'dressed for success'. Maybe they thought I was a foreign cocaine baron? I don't know. Everyone was judging the other by his cover.

A Lesson From A Greek Master

My girlfriend and I also met an interesting guy who lived in Athens. This new Greek friend of ours was the national retailer for the American vacuum cleaners that I had been selling and he had helped us set up our Greek company. He was somewhat older than we were, probably around 65 years old, and his wealth was obvious, since he had employed hundreds of salesmen for many years, selling pots and pans.

He had changed a small apartment complex into his private home. The whole top floor was a huge cognac room. The first floor housed beautiful offices and meeting rooms, and my girlfriend and I slept on the third floor.

During one of our visits, we listened to one of the most impressive sales meetings I have ever heard. It was there and then that I understood why he had become so wealthy. He told me that he really didn't need to do business anymore, but he enjoyed working with younger people. He wasn't doing it for the money but for his admiration of the spirit and fire of the younger generations. He also taught me that you shouldn't chase money but simply strive for good success, because if we are successful, money will follow.

Our Greek friend had many great messages, but there was one in particular that has never left me. He was asking his salesmen how many presentations they had done during the past week and how many vacuum cleaners they had sold. When one of the salesmen admitted that he hadn't done a single presentation, I got uneasy in my seat. I couldn't imagine how this tough veteran of a salesman would handle this situation. Especially since he had told me in the cognac room the night before that you had to love your salesmen but you had to be gut–wrenchingly hard on them at the same time.

So, what was I to expect?

Our Greek friend stopped quietly and stared gravely into the salesman's eyes. Then he browsed the crowd slowly, looking into the eyes of each and everyone, and said in a solemn voice:

"I want you please to pay full attention to what I am about to say. I want all of you to look at this young man as your role model."

The room was dead quiet when he pointed at the young salesman. And I thought that he would finish him off, right then and right there. I couldn't have been more wrong. He continued his speech:

"This guy should be your role model from now on. He was honest with us, telling us things exactly the way they were. Don't bring me lies and excuses. If you really want success, honesty is your most important asset. Now, this week has come to an end, so what we do now is look to the future that is ahead of us and I am convinced that the next week will be even better."

And what do you know?

The following week, this young salesman was the top salesman of them all.

I was seriously impressed with how this sales veteran had managed to find the positive aspect of a poor situation and turn it into his benefit. His message was crystal clear, and every single salesman now understood the importance of being honest.

Honesty, Above All

We had a long talk after this meeting and he told me that everyone of course knew that he hadn't been happy with the salesman and his efforts. But his point was that honesty was still even more important. Of course this is an essential truth, I couldn't agree more. Dishonesty spreads fast, and I'm pretty sure that if I had practiced dishonest methods I would never have been able to offer sales courses and seminars for over 20 years in Iceland.

It's always the fundamentals that count the most, whether we are doing business or just living our lives. Our Greek friend knew this, and he was also aware of how important it is to be able to look forward and see the big picture in the long run. In fact, he was so convincing that he managed to paint a clear picture in my mind that my success in founding the company and selling the vacuum cleaners would be so great that I would be flying around the world in private jets (this is yet to be fulfilled, but it's still on my bucket list!).

In Over My Head

Arriving in Greece was a wonderful experience, but being a foreigner and trying to found a company turned out to be very complicated. Everything was strained and difficult, all processes and procedures took forever, with lots of bumps and bruises. For me, this experience proved the common principle that whatever you plan, it usually takes twice as long with double the costs.

In short, it was a nightmare.

Founding the company proved to be almost impossible. 'Tomorrow' was the answer I most frequently got from the bank, and finally when my bankcard arrived and they had spelled my name incorrectly I got the answer: "Don't matter," which was the second most common answer.

Everything was terribly slow. When our Greek friend asked me if I would be willing to pay under the table and bribe the officials, I simply didn't know what he meant. The discussion faded out, never to be mentioned again, and it wasn't until later that I realized fully what he was suggesting. The rules of engagement are very different between countries. If you want to win a game of chess, you have to play by the chess rules that are in force. You have to know the rules on each tournament, on each location. And there I was, a mildly crazy entrepreneur from Iceland, trying to break into a foreign market that was many times bigger than what I was used to, using the approaches I was familiar with in a completely different culture.

In the end, I managed to found my Greek company. But I never got it fully running and operational. I had built the ship but it never got to leave the harbor.

Nonetheless, I prefer not to to call this venture a failure. I simply ran out of time and money. That was it. I wasn't giving up. I had never learned to give up. But the situation was critical and I decided to take a tough turn and return to Iceland for a sales trip. I simply needed more money.

Back To The Icelandic Reality

This turn took me back to my roots, back to Iceland. And after some consideration, I decided that the remote West Fjords of Iceland would be the market area for me. My plan was to sell a lot of vacuum cleaners and return to Thessaloniki, to my company and my girlfriend and our baby daughter, to continue my efforts in Greece.

It was a dreadful trip, arriving from the warmth and sun in Greece to the bleak and cold Icelandic winter. I was out of money, my dream was hanging from the cliff and the whole situation had become very complicated. Yet, I managed to think to myself: "Yes, the situation is horrible, but it can't get any worse than this." I was determined to turn it around for my girlfriend, my daughter, and me.

I started working immediately on arrival, planning my trip to the West Fjords. This rural, isolated and beautiful area of Iceland was my best chance at success, since very few salesmen had tried selling there before. I was all set to go, having gotten everything ready, but a bad snowstorm hit the area and my flight was delayed. This was nothing to get upset about, because in Iceland we have learned to live with forceful weathers and we are used to all kinds of disruptions to our plans.

Natural Disaster Strikes In Iceland

What happened, however, changed everything, not only my 'important' sales plan but also the whole Icelandic nation. During this storm on October 26th 1995, a huge avalanche hit the small town of Flateyri in the West Fjords. It was a disastrous event, especially since earlier that same year a similar thing had happened in Súðavík, another small town in the West Fjords.

The area was already devastated and the whole nation was too. We had gotten used to avalanches in the past, but they had seldom been this deadly. The Súðavík avalanche had claimed 14 lives in January and grief was still observed when Flateyri was hit. The death toll there was 19 lives, so a total of 33 people had been killed in a span of a few months. The devastation was complete in both of these small societies and it took them years to recover. In many ways, they are still recovering today.

It's hard to write about this kind of scenario and talk about my own situation, so trivial when compared to the pain and suffering in the West Fjords. Nonetheless, I had to reconsider everything I had planned and in every aspect of my life. The West Fjords were out. I had nothing in Iceland, having sold everything when we moved to Greece. And, painful as it was, I had to admit that my Greek adventure was over. I wasn't going to be able to fix the situation and move on with the project.

The Fortune-Teller

A few days before my girlfriend and my daughter arrived in Iceland I was visiting with two friends of mine, Anna and Solla, and they were going on and on about a fortune–teller they had consulted. Supposedly, she was able to see into the past, the present, and the future as well, even sensing deeply personal things about your life.

Of course I just made fun of them, unwilling to believe in this kind of 'magic'. But they insisted I go, warning me that the waiting period could be up to three or four months because she was very popular.

For some reason, I decided to make the call. The fortune–teller answered, telling me that the next available slot was in three months, unless I could come right away, since she had a sudden opening in her schedule. I told her I was in the neighborhood, and what do you know? I was at her doorstep 15 minutes later.

She turned out to be an ordinary, middle-aged woman in a regular apartment building, and nothing about her indicated her hidden gift of fortune telling. She greeted me and seated me in the kitchen, offering a cup of coffee, and then she said:

"I'm going to need a personal item of yours, a ring for example. Or I can use your cup of coffee, after you've held it and finished your coffee."

Cynically, I thought to myself: "Yeah right, so this is actually a cup reading". My faith was weak about this kind of stuff. I was open to the possibility that people could foresee weather conditions or even the alignment of stars, but not that they could predict events from coffee dregs in a cup.

She must have read my mind or sensed what I was thinking, because she said:

"I'm not going to read from the cup. I'm only using it to connect with you. That way, I will receive information and deliver it to you."

That sounded better, but I was still far from convinced. I was very conscious and careful about my body language and especially looking out for suggestive and revealing questions from her. In a word, I was trying to pull a full–blown poker face. She was not going to get any kind of info from me!

But she tried no such thing, no suggestive questions or reading of body language. She simply started making statements about situations that she had no way of knowing, with utter confidence and without hesitation in her voice. This perplexed me, but I tried my best not to let it show.

But then she started talking about my girlfriend and daughter, and that they were in a distant country, a warm country like Spain or Italy or Greece. I then gave up and started believing. She added all kinds of big and small predictions, all of which have already come true in my life and I was utterly amazed by this humble woman.

Not 100% Accurate?

Her only mistake was when she said she was sorry that my girlfriend and I were splitting up. Admittedly, our adventure in Greece had been a strain on our relationship, but we had been together for five years without arguing. She wasn't just my girlfriend but my best friend. We weren't about to split up!

"When things are delivered so strongly to me, like now, they always come true", she added when I was leaving and thanking her.

I didn't argue with her, but of course I thought to myself that, yes she seemed to have a special power, but that she was wrong on this one matter.

My girlfriend would be arriving shortly and my plan was to greet her in a grandiose manner. I booked a fancy hotel suite, bought her 40 long stemmed roses (one for each day that we had been apart) and arranged for a limousine pick–up at the airport. I was full of excitement when I showed up at Keflavík, our international airport close to Reykjavík. But somehow she was less enthusiastic about seeing me. I didn't understand what was going on, but I assumed that she was jet–lagged after the long trip.

On our way home to Reykjavík the atmosphere felt heavy and for the most part I gazed out the window at the bleak and dramatic landscape of the Reykjanes peninsula. This part of Iceland is the first thing visitors notice: not a tree in sight, only black and grey lava with occasional moss wherever you look, the only sign of life being the strokes of steam from the underground heat. In retrospect, if everything had been like it should have been, on our way home I would have taken her to The Blue Lagoon, our fantastic natural spa in the middle of the lava fields that National Geographic has named one of the 25 Wonders Of The World. But that was not to be our path.

We continued our drive towards Reykjavík and she told me that she wanted to go straight to her parent's house. I said OK, but told her that we had to make one stop on our way there, delivering a white lie to keep my romantic plan alive. But when we entered the hotel suite, greeted by the 40 red roses, she acted strange and said she wanted to go to her parent's house. I respected her wishes, and when we arrived there she told me that she wanted a separation.

Split-Up And Back To Grandma

I was in total shock at the time. I probably understood on some level, but was incapable of facing it consciously. And all of a sudden I realized that the fortune–teller had been right about everything. Every single thing. It was beyond my understanding how she could have known this, but there was no denying it, she had been absolutely right. I was facing my most serious blow in life, having lost my girlfriend, my best friend, my business and all my belongings in one stroke.

I was forced to move back with my grandmother, who at this time had reached old age and was also a widow. Everything I had in life could fit into a single bag. After the split–up I had only asked to keep my precious books and audiotapes, but left my girlfriend everything else. The books and tapes helped me survive this period in my life, when I needed all the inspiration and encouragement I could get. The only thing I now had left was my health and my professional knowledge.

I found myself in a small room in my grandmother's apartment, returning from 'almost' conquering the world in Greece. The blow was tough, but the benefits of this turn of events were that I got to spend precious time with my grandmother. We started playing cards and chatting, some nights for many hours. She got to tell me endless facts and stories about her own hardship in life when she, in her early adulthood, started living on a farm with my grandfather. She told me about all the tough living conditions at the farm, the cold and damp air inside the houses and how they had to walk for many miles to get fresh water.

My grandmother really helped me during this recovery. I stayed with her for a long time, mixing together encouraging material from self–help books and strengthening stories from my grandmother about the hardship of other people. One of the books I read and influenced me strongly during this period was You Can Heal Your Life by Louise Hay.

I started to believe that I could also manage to climb out of this low–point in my life. I started to believe that I could do this, that you could do this, that anyone could do it. I started seeing a different perspective, realizing how lucky I had been. I was alive, a horrible avalanche hadn't hit me and I hadn't lost a close family member. Everything seemed a little easier with this way of thinking as the days and weeks passed.

"Never Give Up!"

My grandmother was full of wisdom. But the most important one was this: "Never give up!" She was adamant about this: What doesn't kill you only makes you stronger. And bending and twisting in life, going both up and down, is an essential part of our human existence and our best chance at growing on a personal level.

After a month with my grandmother I moved to a tiny apartment, borrowing a bed, furniture, and some household items from friends and family members. I had already hit the bottom, now the only way was up!

If you ever hit your bottom, just remember that other people have also been there. And they survived. I am not saying that this is an experience that everyone should try! But it's still a precious experience, if you allow yourself to get through it and learn from it. My life has given me many opportunities to fall down and rise again, often being forced to take a few steps back before being able to leap forward again. The heavy blows are the greatest teachers. During difficult times, you must figure out who your friends are, since many of them tend to disappear when the going gets rough.

This girlfriend of mine and I remain good friends today and I don't blame her one bit. I was fortunate enough to have a wonderful daughter with her and for this I am very grateful. The day when my daughter – Sigurlaug Sara Gunnarsdóttir, named after my mother – was born is without a doubt the best day of my life.

Re-Building My Life

It started to become clear to me that in general, people are kind and selfless. This dawned on me while I was recovering. People often go through incredible duress for the sake of others, even strangers, like the countless volunteers and rescuers that participated in the events in Súðavík and Flateyri. Through all these revelations, and through witnessing from a distance the pain of others, I started to get a better and healthier understanding of life and of myself.

This began a period of re-building my life and myself again. I took it slowly, trying to find out which doors would open up instead of which had closed. For two years I continued selling vacuum cleaners in Iceland. I didn't see it as a future project and it was only intended to keep me alive. In this game of life, I experienced a long stalemate, a difficult status quo. I was semi-trapped and I couldn't find a simple way out of the all too familiar business of selling vacuum cleaners. I was good at it, but the passion was long gone.

So, what did it take to break this stalemate? Actually, it was silly pride on my behalf that did the trick. A key manager from the mother company was visiting Iceland and the head of the Icelandic division was taking her out to dinner. I saw myself as a key player in the company's success, so when he didn't invite me to the dinner, I had enough. And when I found out that other salesmen, whom I had taught and trained, were invited instead, I became deeply offended. I thought to myself: "Now is the time to close this chapter and to leave once and for all." I felt a strong urge to extend my knowledge to more people than the ones that were selling vacuum cleaners.

That same night I packed everything I had that belonged to the company and left all documents at the office. I had no idea where I would go next; it was a huge leap of faith. And in retrospect it was exactly the right move in the current situation, putting an end to that complicated chapter of my life.

Something new was about to be born.

Messages From The Middle Of Nowhere

– You never know if the people you meet will become influential people in your life.

– Don't judge people by their appearances.

– Never give up.

– Always dress for success.

– Find the positive elements in every situation and turn them to your advantage.

– Gratefulness for the smaller things in life will bring you more of the big stuff.

– When a door closes, other doors open up.

– It's the hardest blows that teach you the most.

– When you hit the bottom, the only way is up!

– If you are successful, money will follow.

– If you never fail, you have never tried.

– It's not our role in life to understand everything or succeed in everything.

– What doesn't kill you only makes you stronger.

And last but not least:

– Choose to be grateful. It will bring you inner peace, tranquility, and happiness, all of which will come in handy in times of duress.

CHAPTER 7

When You Can Jump Between Europe And North America, You Must Be In The Middle Of Nowhere

From Zero To My Own Sales School

It was on my 30th birthday on a bright and sunny day July 28th 1997 that I decided to launch my career as a sales coach. Of course my plan was ambitious:

I was going to found my very own sales school.

Not many people had faith in me, the vacuum cleaner salesman, nor that I would be able to sell my sales courses to prestigious companies. Let alone that I could profit from this venture! One reason for this is that sales courses were almost unheard of in the isolated market area of Iceland.

I often have a knack for striking into things in the simplest manner. And so I did in this case: I started my career as a sales coach and lecturer by driving around an industrial neighborhood, picking out a Würth retailer, walking straight to the manager and asking him:

"I'm sure that one of your main concerns each day is how

your salesmen are doing?"

"Of course," he replied.

"I am willing to offer you a sales training for all of your staff. I have years of experience in training and motivating salesmen. If you're not happy with the lecture, you pay nothing. That sounds fair, right?"

It only took him a few seconds to reply:

"Sure, that sounds good."

I had managed to secure my first sales training for a company.

Preparing For The Hard Reality

As a part of my preparation I did one open lecture in a small room in the University of Iceland. To fill the seats I simply walked door to door between smaller companies, telling them about the training and offering them to attend. I have a vivid memory of this open lecture and I will never forget it. I had booked some sales chiefs, managers and owners of smaller companies, some of them who knew about me and my previous success, and were curious to hear what I had to say.

One of the attendees was a former schoolmate of mine and he gave me the great idea to dictate my stuff on tape, telling me that he knew a woman who could set everything up profession-ally. For me, this was a huge blessing since I am both dyslexic and dysgraphic, although I have never allowed these shortcom-ings to hinder me in my ventures.

Arriving late, one of the attendees at this open lecture was a young man, casually dressed, his pants sagging in a hip-hop kind of style. He entered into the room that was filled with rath-er stiff business-type men and women, and I could see how some of them looked at him with an expression that said:

"What's this guy doing here? And from what rock did he crawl out?"

I did my best to counteract this attitude during the lecture by giving the young man my full attention and answering all his questions thoroughly. And the only reason I mention this is because this particular youngster, looking somewhat out of place, was so impressed by my lecture that I got many referrals from companies where he had been my advocate, acting completely on his own.

Teaching Everyone ... Everything

Entering the Icelandic corporate market with this novel idea of sales training was quite a challenge. I had to be willing to teach every single training I was offered. It didn't matter if the company was selling products, services, or ideas. And of course this was greatly beneficial because I had to adapt to different circumstances and learn various methods along the way. In a single month, I could be training staff at insurance companies, restaurants, hair salons, mechanics, exporters ...and the list went on and on.

This broad involvement in Icelandic companies made me realize that all the same principles apply, always, no matter what you are selling. Everyone is selling, all the time, and the only question is: How good a *salesman* are you?

Through the years, people have tried to convince me that they are by no means salesmen, privately or professionally. Unfortunately, they have not managed to sell this idea to me.

And that's not all the complications that being a salesman for a living can offer you. I remember, when I was first venturing out, when I told people in Iceland that I was a salesman, people would sometimes ask me why I didn't get a real job. For most people, this was not a real profession, although this attitude changed rapidly over the next years.

Making A Living From My Passion

I really enjoyed this new position of mine, being able to make a living by doing my sales training, through which I got the opportunity to help others, both companies and individuals, to achieve success. I almost felt like I wasn't working because I was simply doing what I love to do. In my opinion, you have a much greater chance of success in life if you do what you love for a living. In this way, you will probably master your profession, whatever the profession is. One reason is that people will pay for passion, for your own passion towards your profession.

So many people today live full and satisfying lives, doing the things they enjoy the most. And in many of these cases, people didn't make a decision to follow their dreams and their passion until they lost their jobs or encountered other major obstacles in life. Something forced them to start thinking about their own life course, something that forced them to ask the imminent question:

What is my purpose in life?

As for me, I am convinced that my purpose in life is to help and encourage other people. This conviction started growing when I started doing my own sales training for companies.

It was on this remote island in the North Atlantic where I realized what my life purpose was. In the middle of nowhere, I started to realize how easy it is in life to overwork oneself but still be underpaid. I wanted to change this, and the change began almost immediately. In a very short time frame, in fact in only two years, my enterprise had grown substantially, and by

September 17th 1999, I was holding my largest single lecture, filling the 500 seats in the City Theatre of Reykjavík with managers and staff from many different companies. Shortly after this event, I was training many of Iceland's largest companies, also the Icelandic banks themselves that were to experience an enormous level of growth a few years later in an era that I cover later on in this book.

Resourcefulness At The Car Wash

Starting out, I naturally had to find my own ways of making my business advance in the right direction. One sunny day I took my car to the car wash. It was a semi-automatic car wash, advancing the car on a belt while the staff cleaned it thoroughly. I have always been attentive towards my cars and their cleanliness, and while I stood and watched the operation through a glass window I started thinking: "I bring my car here once a week. I am paying a ton of money for this service since I like to drive a clean car. How can I arrange something that allows me to come here every week without paying for it?"

At this point, I had to be careful with my spending, even though my training had started to become lucrative. The guys working on my car probably wouldn't be interested in coming to my seminars so I had to find another way. *There must be a way*, I remember thinking.

I approached one guy who looked like a supervisor and asked him if the company was supplying the staff with T-shirts to use during work. He said that they did not, although the staff had often requested it.

"I imagine it would take to a substantial amount of money to buy T-shirts for them all," I said. And he concurred, saying that this was the only reason that he hadn't already done it.

After he had told me that he would need at least 100 T-shirts and sweatshirts because the staff was constantly getting soaked during the workday, I said:

"I have a solution. I will make this happen without you paying a single dollar for it. I will provide T-shirts, sweatshirts, and caps for everyone. In return, I want to be able to bring my car here for a car wash and I also want to put my brand name and logo on the items: SGA Sales School."

He agreed immediately to these simple terms.

This led to the next step: I didn't have a stock of clothes and caps! I picked up the phone and called a supplier, asking for the supervisor for human resources and occupational development. I told the guy that, due to special circumstances, I wanted to invite all his salesmen to a sales training the following week and that he could pay for it with shirts and caps.

He agreed on the spot.

My next call was to Iceland's largest chain of hotels. They, of course, deal with sales every day, just like anyone else. I spoke to a high ranking manager, saying that due to special circumstances I could offer him sales training for his staff. My only requirements were that next week I would need to use one of their conference halls, free of charge.

He agreed to this simple offer.

I was almost there, but I still needed the training material, handouts and more, since this was an extensive training. So, I made a few more calls, closing the deals, one after another.

By the time my car was ready and clean I had already sealed the deal through a few phone calls in the waiting room. Everyone got what they wanted, and I managed to produce a good stack of training material and clothing items that I would use for a long time, even bringing some with me to Africa, which is a story for the next chapter.

Thinking back, this represented my favorite mode of action, simply seeing a problem and taking easy and straight–forward steps towards the solution, involving different individuals that all benefit from the venture.

Realizing My Own Value

In the year 2000, my efforts in sales training had already blossomed, but I was working really hard, almost too hard. I hadn't only secured more clients, they were also much bigger, and I had even managed to raise my price list, now having endorsements and recommendations from numerous individuals and companies. Iceland is a very small country with a tiny market area. Everyone doing business knows everyone else in business, so I only managed this transformation of my business through serious persuasion, using my own sales technique to 'sell' my clients the new price list and why I was now charging more money for a shorter sales training.

It was a complicated period where I was realizing my true worth. And shouldn't we always focus on the value and the built-in knowledge of this kind of service, rather than how long it takes? Would you prefer a dentist that takes an hour to pull your tooth, or his colleague that does the same job in a few minutes? This matter of pricing is a constant part of doing business, because what one client finds expensive, another one considers to be cheap. Price is an abstract concept and it is not a solid indicator of the quality or value of the service. It is actually only a measurement of how much the client values your service. Asking for champagne and caviar and demanding to pay the price of bread simply isn't acceptable. And I would much rather be forced to explain my price list than being forced to make excuses later on because my service wasn't fulfilling to the client. My own motto for a long time has been: "Our mutual goal is your own success"and I am also inclined to agree with Paul "Red" Adair, who once said:

"If you think it's expensive to hire a professional to do the job, wait until you hire an amateur."

Knowing My Place

During this period I also gathered invaluable experience for myself. After a successful sales training course for one of the Icelandic banks, I went to dinner at a top-notch Akureyri restaurant with the manager of the branch and one of the top executives of the main bank. After dinner we sat awhile, an XO cognac in one hand and a Romeo y Julieta Churchill cigar in the other, when he asked me:

– Gunnar Andri, aren't you doing any equity investments?

I was taken aback, simply because of the tone of his voice, indicating that not investing simply was out the question, especially for a guy like me, generating all this revenue. I told him that no, I wasn't.

He blew smoke into the air, full of confidence, and told me not to worry.

– We'll let the bank loan you the money, taking a collateral in the bonds themselves. We know how much money you are making, so you're not a risk for us. Besides, we know that these bonds have a tendency to rise, so the risk should be zero. Be in touch if you want a share in this kind of deal, he added repeatedly.

There are corruption and shady deals in Iceland, just like

anywhere else in the world. And I can't imagine how I would have ended up if I had taken this turn with my life. But I simply didn't. The reason was this: I've always said that you should be in the kind of business you fully understand. Throughout my life I have been involved in all kinds of business ventures, founding companies on my own and with others, even an insurance company. But I simply didn't understand all the twists and turns involved in the business of stocks and bonds and derivatives and the like. I told myself that I simply needed to understand the things I was involved in. And my strength was knowing how to encourage success in sales and business. I simply wanted to share my message to as many people as possible, instead of stepping into financial ventures I had no understanding of.

My Precious P.D.T.D.S Degree

So, my place is my place, even though I was out of place in the eyes of these bankers. And not only in this regard. When the dinner meeting after the sales course for the banks was starting, everyone was introducing him or herself by providing their names and information about their education. Everyone had a master's degree or higher education, so the various abbreviations were flying around: BS, MS, MBA etc. After the round was completed someone decided to ask me about my education, and without hesitation I replied and told them that I was a P.D.T.D.S.

After a moment of silence someone started to try to figure out the meaning of this grand abbreviation. Some were a bit embarrassed about not recognizing this degree of education, others were quick to draw the conclusion that P must stand for 'professor', that the D could stand for 'development', that the T might have something to do with 'training' and that the S must stand for 'sales. After a while I was asked to give the correct answer, and of course they were a bit shocked (and amused) when I told them that P.D.T.D.S. stood for Professional Door-To-Door Salesman.

I respect education deeply, but the fact is that I am almost entirely self–educated. People tend to be surprised when they find out that I don't have a single degree. In turn, my wisecrack about being a P.D.T.D.S. has often led to important discussions on self-learning and self-improvement, because I would argue that a person with an important degree that does not continue to self-improve is far less valuable than an un-educated person that is continuously practicing self-improvement.

My favorite part of the P.D.T.D.S. story? When I decided, for fun, to include this fancy abbreviation under my name in a full-page advertisement in Iceland's largest newspaper!

Gunnar Andri Thorisson

P.D.T.D.S.

The 'Negative' Guy

Once when I was about to start a sales training for an insurance company, Axel, the sales manager, told me that he was having doubts about one of his salesmen. He told me that this particular guy was prone to negativity and damaging comments and that maybe he would have a bad influence on the course and my efforts for other attendees.

I told him not to worry and insisted that if the training didn't work, he would get a full refund.

When the training started, I soon spotted the guy in question, sitting to my right in the classroom. He sat there with his arms crossed and seemed to be distracted with my shoes instead of listening to what I was saying. It was a group of 30 salesmen, and after just a few minutes I heard him say:

"That squeaking noise you are making with your shoes is very annoying."

All the other salesmen exploded at him, yelling that he should mind his own business and shut up. Axel, the sales manager, simply shook his head in a defeated manner. This clearly was 'game over' for him.

I realized that I had to do something drastic, so I stepped closer to the group and shouted at the top of my voice:

"SILENCE!"

Everyone stopped shouting and I got the silence I had asked for. Slowly I checked if the guy had been right about the shoes. And he was; the classroom had a linoleum floor and my shoes had a rubber sole that was making a slight noise.

I turned to the guy and thanked him sincerely for pointing this out to me. I told him that my aim for the day was to sharpen his knowledge about salesmanship and of course this extra noise wasn't going to help him or the others deliver my words to their full attention.

In other words: I admitted my small mistake and told everyone that it wouldn't happen again.

A Defining Career Moment

This wasn't exactly a planned course of action on my behalf. But through this small but defining incident, I started to realize that the guy, called Bjarki, often made sharp and clever remarks.

And when he did, his colleagues got defensive, even though he was often spot-on. The shoes, for example. The noise had also bothered the other salesmen, I later verified, but no one else had the courage to speak out. And even though I had been forced into shouting at the group (an approach I don't generally recommend), the training turned out perfectly and everyone graduated with a smile.

The twist in this story is that when the training was over, the marketing director of the insurance company placed a call to the vocational manager for the Icelandic Savings Banks Federation and booked a meeting with him, on my behalf. This small turn of events was now leading me to one of my largest clients, and none of it would have taken place if not for Bjarki's 'negativity' about my squeaky shoes.

I have told this story in my sales training for many years now, as a part of my method in how to react to criticism.

This is it, in a nutshell:

#1
Give thanks for the criticism.

#2
Admit to the mistake, if there was one.

#3
Solve the problem yourself, or make sure that someone else takes care of it.

As fate would have it, 14 years later a stranger approached me while I was shopping and greeted me in a friendly manner. It took me some time to figure out that it was Bjarki, the 'negative' salesman who had complained about my squeaky shoes. We chatted about old times, recollecting this particular instance together. I am convinced that if I hadn't reacted accordingly to the criticism initially I would never have been offered all the sales courses at the Icelandic banks.

Being In Between

It is in fact an ultra-simple principle: Always be honest and always tell the truth. That way you won't have to try to remember your previous statements. If you always assume that your speech might be recorded and your statements may end up on the cover of the tabloids, then you will always choose truth over false or inaccurate statements in your selling efforts. This, of course, is always important, but especially in my case, being isolated on this island right between Europe and America; this volcanic island where you can see the Mid-Atlantic Ridge, where the tectonic plates of Europe and America are being pulled apart at the rate of approx. 2.5 cm each year.

Each Icelander knows this ridge, since it is beautifully located in Þingvellir, the original location for Alþingi, our parliament. It's one of the oldest parliaments in the world, founded in 930, and is now a national park and one of our most precious attractions. In Þingvellir (the translation is Parliamentary Fields) you can actually walk through the ridge itself in Almannagjá canyon and even go snorkeling in the crystal clear waters of the Silfra fissure that is a part of the ridge.

Þingvellir is simply a beautiful and important place Icelanders. But for me it has always represented something else, too. This ridge for me is symbolic of the choice you have to make between right and wrong, between honesty and deception. And this is particularly important in the business of sales, since we are constantly using information to convince people. You have to choose sides, because otherwise you find yourself stuck deep within the ridge itself.

It really matters which side you are on – which side you choose to be on. On an ethical level, of course, the choice is simple. But on a practical level, it should also be simple, especially in this age of fast information on all the different social media. What goes around comes around, and in the modern world, your bad reputation comes around quickly.

Everyone Is Selling, All The Time

It's true. When you post something on Facebook or other social media, you are entering communication, putting something out there, and hoping for a response when other people are 'sold' to your message. For me, it doesn't matter what your profession is or how old or young you are. The only difference between individuals is how much talent they have in the art of convincing others or how much knowledge they have acquired in this art. No one is a 'born salesman', even though the skill of human communication is a huge benefit in any kind of salesmanship.

In this context, it doesn't matter if you are a carpenter giving advice to a client, a parent raising your children, or a sports coach trying to make your team win a game. CEOs and politicians are in the business of sales on a daily basis, and sometimes I am really amazed at how much mumbo jumbo politicians try to sell us.

I also find it amazing how in politics it seems acceptable not to deliver what is promised. This kind of behavior would never be allowed in normal business transactions and in the sales business. People would simply stop doing business with a company that would behave in that manner and advise their friends and family to do the same.

So, think about this when you are talking to your spouse, a friend, a colleague or anyone else: What is it that you are trying to sell? What are others trying to sell to you?

If I had spoken this frankly about everyday salesmanship twenty years ago, many of my fellow Icelanders would have objected. However, times have changed drastically and I think that today this concept is common knowledge and an accepted truth: We are constantly selling. Some of us are better at it than others, and that's why you will always benefit from quality sales training, both professionally and privately.

If you consider yourself a lousy salesman, just remember the fantastic words of the late Zig Ziglar: "You don't have to be great to start, but you have to start to be great." If you start, you will get results. The results are up to you, depending on how much strength you can find in your life to make the change.

Don't Quit, Just Don't!

Many years ago, I got the following poem as a present. Sources are ambiguous about the author, but was probably written by Edgar A. Guest and published in 1921. The poem struck a chord with me, since its message is that you should never give up. I had it framed at my office for many years:

Don't Quit

When things go wrong, as they sometimes will,
When the road you're trudging seems all uphill,
When the funds are low and the debts are high,
And you want to smile, but you have to sigh,
When care is pressing you down a bit –
Rest if you must, but don't you quit.

Life is queer with its twists and turns,
As every one of us sometimes learns,
And many a fellow turns about
When he might have won had he stuck it out.
Don't give up though the pace seems slow –
You may succeed with another blow.

Often the goal is nearer than
It seems to a faint and faltering man;
Often the struggler has given up
When he might have captured the victor's cup;
And he learned too late when the night came down,
How close he was to the golden crown.

Success is failure turned inside out –
The silver tint in the clouds of doubt,
And you never can tell how close you are,
It might be near when it seems afar;
So stick to the fight when you're hardest hit –
It's when things seem worst that you must not quit.

Remember – it's alright to take a break, but it's never OK to give up!

Messages From The Middle Of Nowhere

– Always think in solutions. Solution is your selling point, whatever the product.

– Everyone is selling, all the time, and the only question is: How good a salesman are you?

– Be in a business you fully understand.

– People will pay for passion, your own passion towards your profession.

– It can take a long time for the rewards of your hard work to be realized.

– Be a smart salesman but always maintain your honesty.

– Don't judge people without knowledge or experience about them.

– Your reputation travels at the speed of light.

– If you always tell the truth, you never need to memorize what you say.

– Most obstacles can be overcome, and most of them lie within ourselves.

– What goes around comes around.

– It's alright to take a break, but it's never OK to give up.

– Never quit, not even when everything seems at its worst.

– If you think it's expensive to hire a professional to do the job, wait until you hire an amateur.

And last but not least:

– You have to choose sides, because otherwise you find yourself stuck deep within the ridge itself.

CHAPTER 8

Aliens In Iceland, Gunnar Andri In Africa

The year 2000 was the year when I came close to giving up. The reason wasn't adversity; it was in fact my own success. I had been so busy doing courses, training, and seminars that I simply needed to rest and recover my energy.

It was a genuine luxury problem.

When I realized this, I started weighing my options. I thought to myself that I could visit my favorite place in Iceland, Hotel Búðir. It is a gem of a hotel, newly renovated and located on a lava field close to the Snæfellsjökull National Park in the western region of Iceland. Only two hours drive from Reykjavík, Hotel Búðir is one of the most beautiful country hotels in Iceland and I would go there regularly to recharge, refresh my ideas and thoughts, and enjoy the stillness of the area and the wonders of the Northern Lights and Snæfellsjökull glacier.

Aliens At Snæfellsjökull

In 1993, Snæfellsjökull became the center of media attention, in Iceland and throughout the world. Somehow it had been predicted that for the first time in history, aliens would land near Snæfellsjökull glacier at 9:07 PM November 5th 1993. Supposedly, this location was ideal because the energy field around the glacier was particularly strong.

Icelanders made the original prediction in connection with a conference on extraterrestrial matters, and the rumor escalated quickly and spread dynamically. The event was covered in every newspaper and every media outlet and Hotel Búðir organized an ambitious schedule for the more than 500 people and foreign media correspondents who waited anxiously (and full of doubt) in the snow and hail on the night of November 5th.

You might have guessed it: No aliens showed up. And to this day, this unlikely event remains a huge mystery. Why did the aliens fail to show? Well, some attendees claimed that the aliens had in fact hovered over the area but decided not to land because of all the fuss and noise and fireworks from the crowd. Perhaps we shall never know.

Charging The Batteries

I realized I had to do something, so I walked into a travel agency with clear instructions:

"I really need a vacation. Please sell me a trip abroad, somewhere different. I want a break from my people. I don't want to meet my fellow Icelanders for a while because they always want to talk about my field of work when I tell them what I do for a living."

I provided the agency with additional information and requirements: It had to be sunny and warm. And new and exotic. With absolutely no cellular connection. Low priced, so I could afford a high standard of living. And beaches, though preferably not the stereotypical ones for tourists.

"Surprise me! Where will you be sending me?"I asked the travel agents.

To my surprise, they immediately and unanimously replied:

"You are going to Gambia in Africa."

Iceland and Gambia seemed like poles apart!

Adventures In Africa

As you can imagine, Gambia proved to be full of surprises for me and for my new girlfriend who went on this magical trip with me. Some surprises were comical, like when I opened my eyes on our private beach and stared straight into the eyes of a local cow! But other events were deeply profound and have stayed with me to this day.

The economy system there was completely different from what I knew and when I was getting to know the locals I realized how absurd I seemed to them. When I was buying beers and soft drinks at the hotel, packing some beverages for shorter trips, they thought I was mad because of the overpricing of the hotel. This wasn't true for me, of course; I was paying much less than I was used to. In my view, they were doing what we often do in our own lives: We tend to confuse our own finances with the finances of others. In their eyes I was some kind of a millionaire.

Gambia is a very poor country, but all I could see was smiling people. This is not to say that happiness comes from being poor.

Far from it; I dislike it when people claim that happiness stems from poverty. In my youth, I got my own share of poverty and its consequences, and I didn't experience much happiness. Of course you can experience certain relief when you rid yourself of financial worries, but that isn't the same as happiness. I believe that happiness comes from within, but at the same time, a person's main objective should always be to become a better and more efficient person, expanding and creating more opportunities for himself and his family.

The Power Of Choice

One thing is certain: Not everyone is given the same opportunities in life to become prosperous. It is unfortunate, however, that so many people do have all the opportunities to create a decent income but do nothing about it. Instead, these individuals use all their energy trying to accept their situation (some even moan and complain about it). For me it's very clear: You can always choose to use your energy to accept your current situation, or choose to take action towards improving it.

Fundamentally, the same laws apply for every person, no matter what their geographical location might be:

#1
What do you do for a living? Are you a CEO at an international company or are you a janitor?

#2
What is your location? What is your situation? Are you located in Africa or Iceland? In a small or a large society? Is the economic situation bad or good? Do you work for a private company or for the government?

#3

How good are you at your current job? It doesn't matter whether you are a salesman, a mechanic, a plumber or a CEO. *Just how good are you?* Remember that there are fewer people to compete with at the top.

#4

How easy or hard is it to replace you? Why should the company you work for pay you more than necessary, if they can easily replace you with an equally qualified employee like yourself?

#5

How good is your social networking? Do you have a large family and group of friends who create a professional network that you can benefit from?

The main law is the basic law of supply and demand. There we find the opportunities. *Is there an opportunity hidden in a potential pay raise?* Can we do anything to make ourselves more valuable as employees in our current marketplace?

I find it remarkable when people tell me what they earn per hour. People don't get paid by the hour, they get paid for their particular contribution to the company or institution, for how much worth they generate.

Eyes Opening

I started formulating many of these ideas and thoughts on my trip to Gambia when I realized how subjective the idea of financial figures and prosperity were between cultures. Whenever I did something that I found natural and unimportant, for example inviting the locals I had met out to dinner, they reacted with surprise and almost became speechless.

I also got to know the daily life of some locals in Gambia and observed how they lived in small society groups where some of the men had more than one wife, sometimes two or even three. When I asked about this arrangement, one Gambian told me:

"One woman, one problem. Two women, two problems. Three women, lots of problems!"

Many Gambians welcomed me into their homes and introduced me to their daily routines. The sister of one of my Gambian friends was christening her infant a few days after we had met. Their home was tattered, but my friend was nonetheless very proud when he showed me an electrical socket, the only one in the whole house. He told me discreetly:

"This is where I sometimes charge the batteries for my Walkman, but don't tell anyone about it, Gunnar Andri".

I enjoyed their hospitality so much that I wanted to buy something for the infant. I pulled out some bills and asked my two private guides what I could buy for this amount.

"We should go and find something for the baby," I said.

To this they replied:

"You really don't have to do this, to spend all this money!"

But on we went and bought all the necessities for the baby: diapers, covers, baby powder, and many more essentials. With the rest of the money we also bought a large sack of rice.

The family was very pleased with these added resources. So pleased, in fact, that they decided to name the little boy after me, using Andri, my second name, as his second name too. I was invited to the ceremony where the boy was christened in front of a large group of family and friends. Of course, the guests had clearly been told who I was so there was a lot of whispering and pointing, especially after some photos had been taken of me with the baby boy. In fact, this commotion reminded me very much of Iceland, where people sometimes like to gossip about their neighbors and the rumors often travel really fast. In a small community like the Icelandic one, it only takes an instant for gossip to spread.

Being in Gambia and being able to give so much was a highly fulfilling experience. One of the things I had taken with me were the caps and T–shirts with the SGA Sales School logo and these got distributed to happy receiving hands.

Scared To Death On A Road Trip

I wanted to travel deeper into Africa and asked the main tour guide if this was safe. I was longing for an adventure. The guide gave his approval and pretty soon we started our journey, driving an ancient Mercedes that was in such bad condition that it would never have been approved for driving on the streets of Reykjavík. One of my personal guides was the driver and he absolutely felt like a true king! We drove out of town, taking gravel roads that in Iceland would never have been considered transitable.

We drove for a while, with nothing but the desert and the wilderness in front of us. Suddenly something appeared ahead. It looked like a car on the side of the road.

I got a little uneasy, suspecting that this might be some sort of planned robbery. As we approached the car, we noticed a man bent over the hood of his car. He didn't look up, which made my girlfriend and I worry. There we were, in the middle of nowhere, I had my Rolex Daytona watch on, and wads of money in my pocket. Would we get robbed, even killed? I know it sounds like silly paranoia, but this is how we felt!

Suddenly the guy looked up, all smiles and cheers.

And what do you know?

On his head was this beautiful cap, with the SGA logo!

As it turned out, the guy only had minor engine problems, so to celebrate the happy ending of our little 'adventure' I proposed that we all go out to dinner. I had gotten my wish fulfilled and the adventure I had asked for. In retrospect, however, this made me realize how powerful a wish can be, but I also learned not to jump to conclusions too fast! Our Nobel Prize author, Halldór Laxness, was convinced that if you believed in ghosts you would find them:

"Strange though it may seem, people rarely show such enthusiasm as when they are seeking the proof of a ghost story—the soul gathers all this sort of thing to its hungry bosom."

This trip to Gambia turned out to be very enjoyable and it also had a profound impact on me on a personal level. I will never forget how annoyed my girlfriend was because of all the insects, especially in the forests. This only goes to show how much an impact a tiny creature can have on the world and its surroundings. You know the scenario: Everything is perfect and you are going to bed with the love of your life lying beside you, until one mosquito begins to buzz through the night.

But here is some good news for you: If you are thinking about visiting Iceland you should know that we don't have a single mosquito in the whole country. And we never have! Maybe the elves or the huge trolls managed to scare them away centuries ago, who knows?

Tiny elements can have a great influence. Iceland is a tiny country and the population is proportionally even smaller: only 330,000 people, as I write this in 2017. I am convinced that it would change your life forever to visit Iceland and see the barren and raw landscapes and experience the ever–changing weather in this country where the glaciers and volcanoes stand in constant conflict.

It's a country where you can feel the forces of nature, even though we don't have any aliens.

Yet.

Messages From The Middle Of Nowhere

– We tend to confuse our own finances with the finances of others.

– You can always choose to use your energy to accept your current situation, or choose to take action towards improving it.

– If you do something that draws attention, you will be the talk of the town. If no one is talking about you, you are simply lacking attention.

– You don't get paid by the hour, you get paid for your particular contribution to the company or institution, for how much worth you generate.

– Remember that there are fewer people to compete with at the top.

– You can always find room for improvement.

– Strange though it may seem, people rarely show such enthusiasm as when they are seeking the proof of a ghost story — the soul gathers all this sort of thing to its hungry bosom. – Halldór Laxness, Independent People

– Learning about different cultures and experiencing them will change your life.

– Be careful what you wish for, you just might get the adventure you asked for.

– Don't be afraid of unknown situations.

– Make sure that you are hard to replace.

– You can't help the poor by becoming one of them – Abraham Lincoln.

And last but not least:

– A single mosquito can change your world.

CHAPTER 9

The Salesman
And The Icelandic
Cat Whisperer

Life can take unbelievable turns and sound like a made–up story. Sometimes we experience strange periods in our lives that really don't make sense, until afterwards. Hindsight somehow always seems to be 20/20.

This certainly applies to the period of my life that I am about to reveal.

It's All About Cats And The IRS

I was on my way to Kattholt, a local shelter for wildcats and stray cats. It's a beautiful place where volunteers feed the cats, take care of them, and find them new homes.

I have always been fond of animals and as a child I had both cats and dogs. One of my favorite activities is horse riding and it is especially enjoyable to ride the Icelandic horse, known world–wide for being a strong riding horse with an extra ambling gait, called 'tölt' in Icelandic.

That day, however, I wasn't on my way to Kattholt because of my love for animals. Believe it or not, I was going there to work, although my reasons for doing so were not so altruistic.

It all started in 2000–2001 when the IRS hit me with all their force.

To begin with, they had made on observation, insisting that I should collect VAT from my revenue from teaching. But that claim was soon withdrawn, since VAT isn't collected from teaching in Iceland and therefore I had been doing everything correctly.

But after that initial and unsuccessful attempt, they hit me again full force, insisting on looking at all my accounting, dating between five and seven years back. I had to turn in all my papers, but I really wasn't worried since I thought I had been doing everything by the book and I had also hired a great attorney.

The case was supposed to be easy and straightforward, but it turned out to be more complicated. My case at the municipal court in Reykjavík received repeated deferrals and was delayed for a long while. At the time, these kinds of cases were rare, but still the authorities took ample time to work on them. As it turned out, the waiting period and the months that followed became a disastrous time for me, privately, professionally and financially. My life was turned upside down in the span of a few weeks. Up until this point I had been busy doing seminars and sales training in Iceland and my reputation was solid. Throughout this ordeal, fortunately, I managed to maintain my reputation, but my finances were crushed.

I had been working a lot for the banks and other big companies and had recently bought a penthouse that was making my monthly payments quite high. This never would have caused me any problems, except for the fact that suddenly my income and my future prospects were filled with uncertainty. In the end I had to give up my wonderful penthouse with a 360° view, overlooking the nearby mountains.

I moved into a tiny rental apartment with Jasmín and Tan-ja, my two Papillon dogs that always made their opinion clear about the people they came across. Whenever someone came to visit, it soon became clear whether they liked them or not, and their judgment was usually accurate.

Victory, But Still A Disaster

To cut a long story short, I managed to win the biggest parts of the government's case against me. But the verdict, however, claimed that I should have collected VAT from a certain field of my services, seeing it as a specialized consulting service, rather than teaching or training.

I don't recall the exact amount that I was sentenced to pay, but before the verdict I was already imagining that the sum would be very high. The Icelandic IRS is authorized to use the maximum interests in cases like this, and I had also heard that they were allowed to estimate the debt by multiplying by ten. The prospects were simply terrible and I was having night-mares about being sentenced to pay a much bigger amount than I could afford to pay. The worst-case scenario would have amounted to several hundred thousand dollars.

Those months were genuinely unsettling, to put it mildly. I didn't know if I should continue doing my seminars and train-ing, and whether I should collect the VAT or not.

In the end, it wasn't too bad. My debt with the tax authorities was fixed at around thirty thousand dollars, which was decid-edly good news. But the bad news was that I didn't own that kind of money. Not by a long shot.

Incarceration ... Or Community Service

The amount was to be paid immediately. My other option: prison time. I considered appealing to the Supreme Court, but I simply couldn't handle another round of waiting for months and months. I wanted to get this over with and move on with my life and my business.

I booked a meeting with the Icelandic Penal Institution, hoping that I would be able to arrange a payment plan. They declined. And when I told them that I simply didn't have the money, they told me that the only option I had left was doing community service to pay my debt.

That didn't sound so bad. At first the official I was meeting with suggested that I could paint some government buildings in downtown Reykjavík. This was a horrible idea, I thought. And I told the official that I couldn't possibly be exposed as a house painter out in the public. At this time, my business had finally started to flourish again; I was managing to build up my seminars and had an ongoing ad campaign in Iceland's largest newspaper, flaunting a full page every week that included a photo of myself.

The official seemed sympathetic about this, and after some consideration he asked:

"How would you feel about feeding cats for a few months?"

Bam! That was it! The deal was to show up at Kattholt cat shelter, two to three times a week for five or six months. It meant 42 appearances, 714 USD per each appearance, 178 USD per hour. What a sweet deal it was, after I had done the calculations!

And to make it even sweeter, I really enjoyed feeding cats and taking care of them, being very fond of animals and pets in general.

Booming Business

At the same time, my business was booming and turmoil was starting, both in the Icelandic business sector and the Icelandic volcanoes (we'll return to that part a bit later in the book). I was in high profile in the media since I was doing large-scale courses for the banks and other big companies. The rise of the 'Financial Vikings' had started, but this was a term coined in the economic boom, referring to our most prominent businessmen that had a habit of going to other countries and taking over lucrative companies and businesses.

I remember that during this time I was often encouraged to take my material and my teaching abroad. My friends kept going on and on about this, saying that I could be successful in other countries. But this wasn't an easy thing for me to do, since I was stuck with my job duty and commitment in Kattholt. Besides, why would I leave my current successful streak in Iceland? The Icelandic króna was also strong against other currencies, so I wouldn't have made more money if I were being paid in U.S. dollars.

My phone was ringing constantly. And of course it didn't stop ringing while I was doing my chores in Kattholt. It always makes me smile, thinking back to those days when I would take a phone call, booking seminars for companies with cats meowing in the background. Sometimes, when I wasn't able to step outside before answering the phone, the person on the other end of the line would ask:

"What's with all the cats around you?"

"Well, I'm not at the office right now," I would reply, and then make up one story or another, involving a lot of cats.

For the most part, I had mastered a good technique avoiding unpleasant cat questions, managing to book meetings and close the deals without having to tell too many white lies. In fact, only a handful of people knew about this community service of mine in Kattholt, while at the same time playing the role of Iceland's number one salesman.

This whole situation was shameful. I was struggling and trying to save face. No one brags about being poor, but everyone is willing to talk about their riches and good fortune. At least I've never met a poor man that is 'proud' to be poor and talks openly about it. On the other hand, I have met many people that have been poor and have managed to enrich their lives. And there is also a great difference between being poor and being out of cash. Poverty is a continuous state of mind while being out of cash is a temporary thing.

This is also how I dealt with my Kattholt situation. I always knew it was temporary. And, to tell the honest truth, I actually thought to myself:

"This will only make my book even better."

A Huge Change In Attitude

It truly was a life–changing experience. One of the things I learned was not to worry too much, especially not about what other people think of you. In retrospect, I don't think that people would have been as shocked as I imagined they would be. Iceland is a very small society, which can prove to be lethal when word-of-mouth starts rolling. On the other hand, being a small society has its benefits. For instance, on a Friday I would maybe have a group of respectable attendees in a seminar, dressed in business suits, but the next night I would meet half of them at the bar or the nightclub where we would dance the night away.

These were crazy times. I was sneaking to Kattholt, feeding

and cleaning cats, while having full-page spreads in the newspapers and other media. You might say that it was a different kind of 'fake it until you make it'.

And that is exactly what was about to happen a bit later. I was in fact on the brink of a huge surge of success.

Living in Iceland at that time was quite colorful, and a bit crazy. Reykjavík was starting to bloom as a tiny cosmopolitan city, bringing ever more tourists into our streets, restaurants and bars. Many of my foreign friends have remarked that the Icelandic nation is a bit like a 330,000 celebs, a nation where everyone thinks they are unique. I think they have a point. Maybe for this reason, when real celebs like pop stars or Hollywood actors come to Iceland, they don't get a special star-treatment and they don't get harassed like they do in other countries. I have met many celebs here in Reykjavík and even raised a glass or two with them. It has always been pleasurable, but never something to consider remarkable. I think it's because we Icelanders are relatively grounded in this respect, or maybe it's because we all consider ourselves to be equally special! I don't know if it's good or bad, but we are a colorful nation, just look at the rooftops of Reykjavík's houses!

My 42 working shifts in Kattholt came to an end. I always showed up punctually, even when I was worn out and tired, because I wanted to pay my dues, and also because otherwise I would have ended up in a prison cell! This helped me realize even more than before that if something is important, it simply has to be done. You just show up and do what is necessary, and in my case, I decided from the start not to view the situation as negative. Not for a minute did I brood in a negative way.

Getting To Know Network Marketing

My business was booming and I was on a streak. Not only was I paying my dues to society, but also my sales courses were in full swing. At the same time, I was on the lookout for new business ventures and was starting to consider network marketing. I wanted to get a first hand experience from this sector of business, simply because I knew that in Iceland the market for a specialized sales expert wasn't big enough. If I wanted to stay in Iceland and continue with my career as a lecturer and advisor, I knew I had to improve my capabilities and areas of expertise.

I started by reading every book on network marketing (or multi–level marketing) I could put my hands on. I even educated myself while feeding the cats in Kattholt, listening to audio lectures and audio books, building up my own capabilities and knowledge.

I am a fan of network marketing and continuous revenue business for many reasons. I am especially fond of how network marketing can give individuals a chance to grow and learn, the reason being that in network marketing, so many other individuals will benefit from your own success. The knowledge is therefore passed on. It's also important to find both a product and a company that you genuinely want to connect with, a company you actually believe in.

I say this, even though once I took part in a network marketing company that went out of business after I had spent a whole year working on it from my end. Through this I have learned that it doesn't matter what people actually do for a living; whether it is a business venture or something else, the fundamentals are always the same:

If something is meant to be, it's always up to you. You are in control. Start by improving yourself and your side of things, start doing and then you will have success.

Be. Do. Have.

The Key Ingredient

When you listen to a lot of audio books or successful lecturers you start to detect a certain pattern, no matter if it's related to sports or business, no matter who it is or what country the lecturer comes from. The elements of this pattern can perhaps be summed up like this:

Your own attitude is a key ingredient to your success. You will fail at least once on your way to the top. Learn from your own mistakes, but also learn from other people's mistakes. And last but not least: Always keep your heart and mind open to improvement and new knowledge.

That was the main reason I decided to dive into network marketing. To learn. And one of the things I learned rather quickly is that people who aren't successful at network marketing are usually successful at finding scapegoats for their lack of success. They claim that the product isn't good enough, that the company is lacking, and they find a thousand other excuses. This is a dangerous path, since it's a universal law that the only thing you can really control is your own attitude. Other people, places and things are simply out of reach.

When I was studying network marketing I continued doing seminars and sales training, but I also began publishing my own material. I started with a two CD audio book in Icelandic called 55 Tips For Better Service. I worked on the script for a long time, showed up at a professional studio and dictated the whole thing. I never thought it would be a problem, reading some text out loud? But I found out the hard way how straining this line of work is, and it took me a long time and much effort to do it. This increased my respect for professional and full time lecturers and I also began to realize why more people in Iceland weren't doing the same thing I was doing.

I started to realize that I was good at what I did. And I also realized that I should be grateful when my projects were hard work, because it kept the losers away! It's good to remember this:

> *Tough times never last, but tough people do.*
> Robert H. Schuller

Success Through Helping Others

So, there I was, prowling around, trying like an Arctic Fox to find every little element that would help me survive. My circumstances weren't all that great, but I was trying to overcome my difficulties. And as so often is the case, helping others was a big part of my solution, even though I never imagined that I would eventually make any money on the venture. Around Christmas 2003 my company, SGA, became a sponsor for the newly founded theatrical group Fimbulvetur. Their mission was to stage a play called *Christmas 2* by Jeff Goode. My role as a sponsoring partner was to provide advertising money and a website for the group.

During this period I got to witness firsthand how hard it is for an amateur theatrical group to cover the marketing elements properly and to compete with the professional theaters in Iceland. So, I started wondering how I could bring the theater closer to the public and at the same time make it easier for both amateur and professional theaters to promote themselves.

This lead to a small epiphany on January 27th 2004 when it dawned on me that the proper place for this kind of initiative was, of course, the Internet! It didn't take long for me to confirm that the domain www.leikhus.is was available ('leikhús' means theater in Icelandic, but the literal meaning is 'playhouse'). I bought the domain without any hesitation and started working hard. The preparations took a few months, in June the Beta version was launched and in autumn 2004 we officially opened a comprehensive site with everything you need to know about Icelandic theater. My company, SGA, is still the proud and primary sponsor of leikhus.is.

I bring this up because countless pleasant things have come my way because of this initiative, such as continuous interesting and fun people, artists and other talents. It's unfortunately a common occurrence for artists to forget about marketing and sales techniques. In an ideal world, an artist wouldn't need to 'brand' himself, but that is not true in the real world. In my opinion, you have to spend time on marketing, branding and sales, also and equally so if you are simply an artist trying to make a living. It has always about selling your ideas, bringing them forward, allowing them to reach larger audiences. Leikhus.is originated as a mixture of my own passion for theater and my newfound (but ever so much alive today) passion for websites. I didn't think about leikhus.is as a business venture and as a source of income; for me it was all about visibility and equal opportunities for smaller theatrical groups. For 14 years, my site has been operating smoothly, managed by myself and other theater experts, and running solely on advertising income. It is still the only place where you can find all the info about Icelandic theaters and show times in one place.

What Is The Origin Of Success?

The fact is that if I hadn't taken that leap 14 years ago, I am convinced that I wouldn't be doing as much online business as I am doing today. It was a stepping-stone, created in an altruistic gesture. My point is: sometimes the things you do simply for passion lead you towards other lucrative opportunities. It's a matter of insight, and of listening to that inner voice that says:

Jump!

And almost all the time, jumping is the right thing to do. If you have your instincts aligned correctly, you are like a Viking who is able to navigate between countries and continents, using only the stars. It's a matter of reading the signs, both within ourselves and in the world around us.

When I was launching leikhus.is, I was also very busy doing lectures and seminars. But I also took an unexpected dive: I suffered a financial blow when a close friend of mine betrayed me. I was even forced to move. I had practically nowhere to go, I had no money for a down payment, so I was forced to rent a tiny apartment.

I went online, trying to figure out how to recover and be able to buy my own apartment again. While I was browsing real estate, I stumbled upon an office space located just outside Reykjavík. The price was right and I could visualize how easy it would be to change this space into an apartment, thus raising the price substantially. I was then living in postal code 101, the fantastic favorite downtown area of Reykjavík where I am still living today, but my instincts told me to stay in my tiny apartment, refurnish this office space and make a good profit in a few months. And this I did. Through some special deals (and good salesmanship) I managed to buy the asset for a very fair price, despite my lack of money at the time of purchase.

And lo and behold! After refurnishing, I found tenants that rented the apartment. And only six months later I had resold the apartment with a profit so high that I was able to buy myself a 200 sqm office space in a penthouse on Laugavegur, the main shopping street downtown. Getting the licences needed to change this space into an apartment had its struggles, but I managed eventually.

It was a ride, to be honest! Six months earlier I had taken a serious financial blow and I was living in a tiny rental apartment, but now I had made myself a fantastic nest in a penthouse with a five meter ceiling height in downtown Reykjavík. With a bit of creative thinking and resilience, I would later be offered 2 million USD for this same apartment.

When you get hit, sometimes it's the beginning of something fantastic, though it may be hard to see it like that. There just might be a tiny grain of truth in the saying that when one door closes, another one opens up.

Or, as someone put it:

Karma goes something like this: First the birds eat the worms. Then the worms eat the birds.

Everything goes around and comes around, and we never know exactly where we are in this eternal cycle.

Enjoying the ride is therefore our only healthy option.

Enjoying the ride and never giving up.

Messages From The Middle Of Nowhere

– If something is important enough, it simply has to be done.

– The only thing you can control is your own attitude.

– Tough times never last, but tough people do.

– Sometimes the things you do simply for passion, lead you towards other lucrative opportunities.

– Helping others can create great opportunities.

– When you get hit, sometimes it's the beginning of something fantastic.

– Anger and other negative emotions can be used for your benefit.

And last but not least:

– If you have your instincts aligned correctly, you are like a Viking who is able to navigate between countries and continents, using only the stars.

CHAPTER 10

The Birth Of
The Viking Sales King

The HIVE Sales Adventure

Early in 2005 I received a phone call from a young guy that told me he was a sales and marketing director for HIVE, a new phone and Internet provider. He wanted to meet me and said that he and his company needed some advice and tips.

A few days later, I showed up for a meeting and was greeted by two young guys. They explained to me that they were selling Internet connections and that their future plan was to offer their customers the whole communication package with a landline phone, mobile phone and Internet connections. Their main focus was ADSL connections. They had mostly been selling through the Internet and through incoming sales calls to the help desk, and the result was a small office/shop that was doing okay.

They also told me that they were interested in selling their ADSL connections through cold calling, but they had already tried using several sales companies and none of them had delivered any impressive results, despite charging full price for their services.

At this point in the meeting one of them pulled out a printout of a script for cold calling. They were clearly very proud of the document and told me how much work they had put into it, and then they asked me to read it over and tell them if anything needed to be amended.

Taking A Firm Stand

I glanced over those few pages and instantly saw they were completely useless. They didn't know what they were doing, that much was obvious. I wondered for a moment whether I should tackle the situation in a soft or a hard way, and then I put my right hand over the document on the table, pushed it aside and said:

"Forget this script! It's useless. This approach will never work and it will never result in any decent sales figures!"

They looked at me, rather shocked, not knowing how to react to my outburst. After a while, one of them, Thorsteinn Friðriksson, replied:

"So, what should we do? What do you propose, if our approach is no good?"

"I want a meeting with you, the company's owners and the CEO," I replied.

They agreed, and the meeting was arranged for the following day.

Old Connections Can Suddenly Pay Off

The attendees were the sales director, the marketing manager, the CEO and I. The CEO looked rather familiar to me but I couldn't recall where from. Then he said:

"We have met once before, when I was chatting to Aðalsteinn outside his company. We exchanged words for a few minutes."

"Okay, great," I said. "Was it Aðalsteinn that recommended me?"

"Yes, that's right. And you came highly recommended."

This led our conversation towards how Aðalsteinn and I had met in Nice, France over 20 years earlier. My childhood friend, Örn, and I had stumbled upon a private beach where Aðalsteinn and I had a long conversation about sales strategies. I found it fascinating that 20 years later, my sales pitch at the beach was returning as a potentially huge project.

After some initial exchange of thoughts on the matter, the CEO asked me:

"So, what are your recommendations? What we have been doing up until now hasn't been working. Your reputation is quite good. How would you approach this?"

I allowed myself to pause before I answered, looking him straight in the eye. When I saw that his curiosity had increased, I finally replied:

"What sales numbers would you want to see from selling ADSL connections through cold calling from your staff?"

He thought about this for a few seconds:

"For us, it would be a huge success if new sales through cold calling would amount to 10% of the ADSL connections we are already providing and have sold through our website and our support desk."

I looked him in they eye:

"Great. We have a deal. I can do this. I will share the risk with you. I will not send you sky-high bills, except if the results are exceptional, but then it will be well deserved anyway and you will pay with a smile on your face."

Going All In

I was taking a huge risk, deciding not to use my time for lucrative seminars and sales training. The venture therefore simply had to become a success, in order for me to benefit from it. This experience most likely had an enhancing effect on my personal motto: Our common goal is your success. The great Zig Ziglar put it like this: You can have everything in life you want, if you will just help enough other people get what they want.

My offer to HIVE was a certain minimal sales percentage from all ADSL phone sales. If the initiative were successful, I would also receive additional bonuses, a percentage of the company's turnover. To nail the deal I said to them, rather boldly:

"What I am about to do with you, and for you, is simply to do what I do best. I will provide sales counseling, I will teach and train your designated salesmen and also give lectures to the rest of your staff. Everyone will know how to sell. And to make myself clear: My job will not include standing in front of the copying machine or making coffee. I consider all my time very valuable to your company and will therefore only do the jobs that I am best at."

I firmly believe that we shouldn't do everything ourselves, that we should delegate and get assistance so we can focus on doing what we do best.

We started by making a three-month deal, an arrangement that was later to be renewed twice, making this sales initiative last a total of nine months. Together, Thorsteinn and I, along with other executives, decided to think big and make a sales call to every single home in Iceland. This was equal to a declaration of war against the large companies, Vodafone and Síminn (the oldest phone company in Iceland, formerly run by the government).

From 10% To 80%

It was a very bold move. Crazy, even. And how did it go? Well, the initial plans were to make ADSL connections a 10% part of the total income.

When we finalized the project, the number we had reached was 80%.

Not to brag, but it was a massive success. After this, I could indisputably be named the Sales King of Iceland! I had money flowing out of my pockets and, for a long time, I could pick and choose the companies I wanted to work with, just because of the reputation of this project.

The company of course was forced to pay me large sums of compensation and bonuses. But they did it with a smile, like I had predicted. In just a few months, I had turned this small business into a major player against the big companies.

Many elements contributed towards this success. I got to be the sole source of experience and knowledge, meaning that every single staff member was personally trained by me, both the general staff, the sales group, and even the executives them-selves.

Discipline, Enthusiasm, And Honesty In Every Sale

The training started in small meetings where I would coach the staff and teach them, word by word, how to make a successful sales call. I told them over and over again what to say and what not to say. Instead of providing them with a script I went the opposite way. I didn't allow them to take any notes during these training meetings. Instead, I would make them repeat the pitches and the phrases, first up against one another and then up against me, where I would play the role of a very difficult customer.

I maintained a strict discipline, much stricter than I had done before. I told them that if they failed it would be my business and reputation on the line. I urged them to trust my approach and to follow my dos and don'ts in a rigorous manner. I also told them that if they complied, they would earn more money than they could dream of.

And everything went as planned.

These were mostly very young people, and they were willing to learn. What they gained was superb training, hands-on experience, and many of them managed to earn thousands of dollars each month, often just doing a part time job alongside their college studies.

Everything didn't always go super smoothly, however. It took a great effort on my behalf and I had to constantly remind them and myself of the importance of the project. I would listen in on their sales calls and correct them directly afterwards. I would create all sorts of crazy sales competitions with various incentives and awards. The top five salesmen were picked up at their houses in a limo and driven to my place where we would drink champagne on the balcony of my penthouse in Laugavegur. It was an all–in experience where the limo waited for us and took us wherever we wanted to go, to the restaurants, bars or clubs.

And the top ranking salesman? His main reward was this: He was allowed to make his sales calls from the CEO's office. There was a sacred rule that everyone adhered to: no one was allowed to touch the CEO's chair except the leader each time.

I would walk between the salesmen, waving wads of cash in their faces, creating an atmosphere of hungry wolves. But amidst this fabricated craziness, I would also monitor the ethics of the sales crew. I wanted honest sales or no sales at all, and I made it very clear that anyone that tried to use false information in a sales call would be fired immediately. Honesty must always precede success.

The Wolf Of Reykjavík? Maybe Not ...

In a way, it was a softer kind of Wolf of Wall Street scenario, and years later I even got to meet Jordan Belfort at a private party that was held after his lecture in Iceland in May 2014. He walked up to me and starting chatting, so I asked him with a smile if he wasn't afraid to be there, surrounded by original Vikings. He looked at me, not fully understanding my words.

– What do you mean?, he asked.

– I'll show you what I mean, I replied, grabbed him gently but firmly under my arm and wrestled him down to the floor. This wonderful moment was even captured in a photo. It was, of course, just a prank and Jordan, being an easygoing guy, enjoyed it. I also gave him a copy of the book Against The Grain (co–written with Brian Tracy and other authors) since one of the main messages of my chapter had been:

No one is taller than you, no one is bigger than you, and no one is above you.

HIVE was a fantastic adventure and it will always make me proud. I was allowed to make a small company grow immensely and I also got to influence a large group of young salesmen, many of which have themselves developed successful careers.

The End – Beginning

Success isn't always the best way to learn and mature. In 2006, everything went perfectly. I was on a roll. My schedule was filled with lectures, sales training and also with private consulting jobs, similar to HIVE, where I would get percentages from sales. It was party time in Iceland and I was enjoying the fun.

I was so busy that I was forced to say no to some exciting projects. Ever since I started this career of mine, my market share in sales training has been significant. And I'm proud to say that honesty has been a key factor in this success. Other individuals or companies that have tried to compete against me have given up rather quickly. In this kind of micro-market environment, you must have substance, because your bad reputation spreads like wildfire.

By this time, the economic boom was in full swing in Iceland. The real estate business was particularly crazy and basically anyone could become a real estate agent; they only had to check whether you had a pulse and if you were actually breathing.

Did I take part in this feast of prosperity?

Yes, I did.

It was fun, but the lessons to be learned from this period only dawned on me much later.

The Big Boom In Iceland

Today, I can understand how careful you have to be when this kind of success prevails in society. But in 2007, I wasn't careful enough. Actually, no one was. The financial sector grew and grew, becoming larger than the fishing industry in Iceland. Only a handful of politicians and some foreign specialists and journalists were starting to warn us that the situation was unstable. We didn't listen to them. We didn't want to. We just wanted to hear the sound of high–flying money.

While we are on the subject of flying high, I want to add a story about Óskar, a dear friend of mine. Óskar was a prominent businessman in Iceland and a dear friend, but sadly he passed away way too early, at only 48 years of age.

Out of the blue I received a phone call from Óskar on a Saturday morning:

"Pack your toothbrush, we are dining out."

I was pleased, but not surprised at all. Óskar was always full of surprises and during these years we knew how to party, living by the profound motto 'It's fun to have fun!' This particular day I thought to myself that perhaps he was taking me to the town of Akureyri, the capital of North Iceland. He had flown us there on numerous occasions to go to Sálin hans Jóns míns concerts. 'Sálin' was Iceland's #1 pop group for many years, although foreign readers will now be much more familiar with Björk, Sigur Rós, Of Monsters And Men, Gus Gus, Kaleo and many other fantastic Icelandic bands.

But no, it wasn't Akureyri we were headed to.

Óskar was taking us to The Faroe Islands – a cluster of small islands located halfway between Iceland and Norway where only 50,000 people live.

My girlfriend and I showed up at the airport and there we found Óskar and his girlfriend in a 20-seat airplane. We took off and opened the first bottles of Champagne. Upon approaching The Faroe Islands we were told that the weather conditions for landing were probably dangerous due to a bad forecast. Trying to wait out these conditions, the pilot hovered around the islands for 30 minutes, hoping for the best. But our fuel was running low and we had to make a decision. I told Óskar that returning to Reykjavík was out of the question. We didn't have enough fuel to head for another country, so our best shot was flying to Akureyri. The pilot announced our arrival to air traffic control, and they also managed to contact the finest restaurant in Akureyri on our behalf, and because of our special request, they kept the place open for much longer than usual and the owners themselves both cooked our meals and served our tables. Of course we drank Champagne during the whole flight and also at the restaurant. Champagne became somewhat of a standard beverage during those years. The day after that adventurous night, we flew back to Reykjavík after an unforgettable one-day trip that had cost us around 20,000 USD.

We didn't mind the cost. We had the money and were simply living the dream to the fullest, like so many were doing around us. After this trip I have often thought to myself:

Life is full of detours and it can seem confusing, but in the end, you sometimes end up in your original destination.

A Feast For A Forty-Year Old, But The End Was Nigh

In 2007 I had potential and determined investors that wanted to buy my penthouse. The estimated sales price was 2,000,000 USD. Yes, that's how crazy those times were. I was living in one of the largest penthouses in Reykjavík but despite that crazy offer I didn't find it tempting enough to sell.

July 28th 2007 was my 40th birthday. I was at the peak of my success and considered myself to be rather modest when I invited around 70 people to a birthday party in my penthouse. A further indication of the mind-set during these years: I hired security guards to welcome my guests, in full suits with weapon detectors. This was a ludicrous scenario in Iceland, where the ratio of gun murders per capita has always been very low, almost non–existent. This was just my way of creating an atmosphere to kick the party off in an unusual way.

I had hired chefs, waiters and a piano player to make everything just right. My girlfriend surprised me, and everyone else present, by getting an Indian dancer to perform a fantastic live show. Friðrik Ómar, a popular Icelandic singer, remixed a song for me with brand new lyrics, with a chorus that belted out: "Money … money … money!"

Yes, the Champagne was flowing indeed, and at this point no one could have suspected that the end of all of it was coming. No one suspected that very soon I would be forced to sell my 2,000,000 USD penthouse on a flash sale. I had no idea how dire the situation had become in the Icelandic financial sector.

No one did.

I never would have suspected the events that would unfold during the next year. I had ongoing business deals with almost all the largest companies in Iceland. They were based on trust, instead of pre-paid service deals. Everything was to be paid afterwards. That was the plan.

And then, everything collapsed.

Messages From The Middle Of Nowhere

– Focus on solutions, rather than problems.

– Be careful when your success is peaking.

– Don't be an expert on everything. Ask for help and delegate sub–projects.

– Always treat everyone kindly. You never know where your next recommendation comes from.

– If you truly believe in the project, take a chance!

– You can have everything you want in life, if you help others get what they want. – Zig Ziglar.

– No one is taller than you, no one is bigger than you, and no one is above you.

And last but not least:

– Learn how to read into the warning signs around you.

CHAPTER 11

God Bless Iceland, And Our Savior, Eyjafjallajökull Glacier

It was early 2008 when I started to notice warning signs around the corporate landscape in Iceland through the large companies I was still working for. More and more companies started paying their bills late. I had substantial amounts in accounts receivable, but still I kept thinking that these were reliable companies, and that I shouldn't be concerned.

Something Was Rotten In The State Of Iceland

As the months passed I began to feel mixed emotions, without fully realizing why. In retrospect it's easy to see that something was boiling underneath the surface and that a storm was approaching. And maybe I simply wasn't open to the signs. No doubt I had lost the ancient ability to predict the weather as my grandmother had. Reading into the clouds, that's how people survived back then. Also by relying on popular wisdom, like this saying: "Fátt er um vinina þegar ölið er af könnunni." It translates to: "Your friends become sparse when the ale runs out." Maybe you know the feeling? Success brings you a lot of friends, but when the going gets tough, a lot of them also get going.

So, I had no idea that a monster storm was about to hit Iceland, an economic 'natural' disaster of giant proportions. I was running my operations on full power so I didn't have the time or the perspective to see the warning signs clearly, for example, the incredible number of construction cranes that stuck out in the small city landscape of Reykjavík. The expansion was enormous, the cost of things didn't matter anymore, and it was just a matter of getting things done, right here, right now! Somewhat clueless, I imagined that for me this would make 2008 my most lucrative year since I started doing business.

To be fair to myself, I at least had an inkling of what was about to happen. For example, on August 7th 2008, I decided to start a new business venture by buying the domain www. 2fyrir1.is, a 2 for 1 coupon site offering special deals. Given the atmosphere in society, it was an odd move, and people around me rather frowned upon it. "Icelanders don't like fishing for discount offers, especially not with coupons," they said. This was true, but it was also about to change very fast.

Collapsing Icelandic Banks

Only two months later, on October 6th 2008, the government imposed a special emergency act that overtook all three major banks in Iceland. This regulation happened overnight and the day after, everything changed. Geir H. Haarde, then prime minister, had addressed the nation the day before in a dramatic television address that the whole nation watched in awe. He commented on how the scope of the Icelandic private banks had become too big, much larger than the GDP of Iceland, and that if they were to collapse they could threaten the whole Icelandic economy and the result could be a national bankruptcy.

Haarde concluded with these famous last words: "Guð blessi Ísland."

God bless Iceland.

Our country was obviously in huge peril.

It was a dramatic way of finishing his speech, since Iceland is generally a secular nation and we usually don't make reference to religion in such a manner. It was also apparent from the tone and trembling of his voice that things were extremely serious.

It was a disaster, not a natural one but a man-made disaster.

A Country Used To Natural Disasters

Now, it may be added that living in Iceland entails many imminent threats. We are used to living in the shadow of dramatic events and we are also used to dealing with them. Two years after this man-made disaster collapsed Iceland, another kind of natural disaster first shook the country and then the whole world. But this disaster was actually going to have a profound impact on the economy, as years passed on.

I am, of course, referring to the infamous volcanic eruption in Eyjafjallajökull glacier in March 2010. It had a huge impact on millions of passenger flights all over Europe. Large amounts of ash were blown out of the volcano for many days, and due to international safety regulations, a large number of flights within, to, and from Europe were cancelled, creating the highest level of air travel disruption since the Second World War. This caused great turmoil in Europe, but eventually it had the effect that many people took interest in our peculiar volcanic island in the North Atlantic. This created a huge boom in tourism that is still making our economy thrive today.

The general public was taken by surprise by this eruption,

but the specialists weren't surprised at all. They had seen the warning signs around the area for many days before the eruption.

Nonetheless, Eyjafjallajökull is just a dwarf of a volcano compared to the volcano Katla. There lies a true threat to us Icelanders, and maybe the whole of Europe. History tells us that every time Eyjafjallajökull has erupted, Katla has followed a few years later. These two volcanoes are located close to one another, and research has shown that lava from Eyjafjallajökull could possibly reach Katla's lava chambers and spark an explosive eruption. Nothing is for certain, of course, but the odds seem to be even greater if we consider that Katla hasn't erupted for an unusually long period of time.

The Queen of Icelandic volcanoes however isn't Katla; it's Mount Hekla, one of the most active volcanoes in Iceland. The myths that have surrounded Hekla through the ages have been countless, and centuries ago it was commonly believed that Hekla was the gateway to Hell itself.

If that isn't true, well, at least we can say this: If Hekla starts erupting, all hell will break loose. Not just for Icelanders but also for many European nations. And she probably will. Huge volcanoes have a tendency of exploding on a regular basis.

Just like our economy.

Don't economic recessions seem to have almost a fixed interval? Maybe it's just part of life's tempo, rising, falling, rising again, falling again? Never a straight line, unless you are dead and buried?

In any case, life seems to involve endless contrasts and conflicts, fire and ice, victories and defeats.

And in October 2008, everything seemed to be taking place at the same time, the rising and the falling and the losing and the dying. It was a life–changing experience where many rooted ideas simply came to pass. As a nation and as individuals, we had to rethink everything.

The Big Nationalization

On October 7th, the day after the television address, the government institution FME (The Financial Supervisory Authority) took over the Landsbanki bank and two days later it took over Kaupþing bank. Both of these banks had become huge players in the global banking sector.

Glitnir, the third Icelandic bank, had been taken over on September 29th. In a way, this chain of events started with the fall of Lehman Brothers earlier in September, since Glitnir relied heavily on lines of credit from Lehman Brothers.

I still remember when I heard about Glitnir for the first time. I was getting the tires replaced on my jeep when a customer said to another:

"Have you heard the news? Glitnir has fallen."

I thought to myself *'what the hell is happening?'* and I instantly had a sinking feeling about it. I called my co–worker who did my accounts and told her the news.

"Don't worry about this, Gunnar Andri. Everything will be just fine."

"You know that generally I am optimistic, but I'm starting to think that everything is going down the drain," I replied.

Watching the news that same night, a foreign friend of mine that was visiting said to me:

"Gunnar Andri, what's with that look? I've never seen you like this before."

"We are going down. I can sense it. This is the beginning of something big, something that will take us years to recover from."

Unfortunately, my instincts were absolutely right. Landsbanki and Kaupþing were taken over and the entire Icelandic economy came close to full collapse. For days, people stopped moving. They just stayed at home, recovering. And after that, nothing was the same. Numerous companies witnessed their income fall drastically, and large numbers of people lost their jobs during the next weeks and months.

Revolt And Fires In Peaceful Reykjavík

In my high–end consulting business, I didn't just experience a decrease in income.

I went directly from ON to OFF. It was a complete shutdown of all my ventures.

The business of sales was dead and all my receivables from the large companies were lost money.

I was both devastated and angry, like almost every Icelandic citizen. Directly after these initial events, people started demonstrating in front of Alþingi, our parliament at Austurvöllur, the heart of downtown Reykjavík. People demonstrated on and off, and these protests culminated in January 2009 when the force of the demonstrations was so intense that the government was forced to resign, allowing for a temporary minority government to run the country and hold premature elections on April 25th 2009.

For the most part, the protests were peaceful. Despite our Viking heritage, we are not accustomed to carrying weapons of any kind, so people simply brought all sorts of cutlery, pots and pans to bang on and create as much noise as possible. The rhythm was heavy because the people were genuinely affected, frightened, and hurt.

These protests were named Búsáhaldabyltingin; 'búsáhöld' means 'kitchen utensils' but it was referred to as The Pot and Pan Revolution in English. The protestors had two main demands. They wanted resignations and new elections, and they wanted Davíð Oddsson, the former prime minister and key player in the build–up of our oversized banking system, to step down as Governor of the Central Bank of Iceland, after some of his actions were deemed questionable. When both of those demands were met, the protests settled down, though we have had intermittent protests over other matters since.

Although it was non–violent, it was totally crazy. We had a huge, angry crowd banging on our parliamentary building, the breaking of windows, some injured policemen and even open fires in Austurvöllur. During those intense days before the government resigned, the smell of fear and burning wood hovered over Reykjavík.

The Terrorist Act And The Icesave Dispute

Watching the news during this time was particularly painful because of the so–called Icesave bank accounts that Landsbankinn had founded, mostly in the U.K. and the Netherlands. These accounts and circumstances would lead then British Prime Minister Gordon Brown, to enforce their Terrorist Act against us, putting Iceland on a list of terrorist states. This was not well received by Icelandic politicians and the public. The debate revolved around a private bank that had now collapsed, and British officials were now trying to get the Icelandic public to pay for it.

I always found this to be a strange kind of logic. None of

us had signed an agreement to vouch for the ventures of these banks. It took years to resolve this Icesave dispute, and it divided the nation. In April 2011 the current government offered the nation an Icesave agreement (named Icesave III), but Ólafur Ragnar Grímsson, President of Iceland, refused to sign the agreement and sent the matter to a referendum. We had a 75% turnout and the agreement was declined. This led to an even more complicated process, involving the EFTA Surveillance Authority and its final ruling, years later, eventually was very positive for Iceland.

So, we were right about saying no to the agreement with the help of our president. In this semi–war between Iceland, Britain, and the Netherlands, we didn't allow ourselves to be forced or bullied. We are a small but strong nation, and justice did prevail eventually.

Back To The Drawing Board

On a personal level, a month had passed since the first days of the collapse. It was November, and nothing was happening for me, business–wise. I had to do something.

So, I pulled the discount website out of the bottom drawer and started working on it. I didn't have time to sulk over having lost a chunk of money and lots of business. The new situation in Iceland was that many families had been forced into poverty, at least temporarily, and this created grounds for my new venture. Everyone was holding on to their resources and companies had to find new ways to find customers and create business for themselves.

For most families, monthly payments were doubled or tripled, mostly because of housing mortgages rising when our currency collapsed and due to the fact that many Icelanders had taken foreign currency loans in the months leading up to the collapse. All necessities also became more expensive. It was like being on a burning boat, striving and struggling just to keep it afloat. And me? I was one of the fortunate ones, because I had all kinds of stuff I could liquidate, like Rolex and Breitling watches and all kinds of expensive items I had accumulated through the years.

But it wasn't enough. No matter how much I paid, everything kept getting more expensive. And during this time I would sometimes think: "Why didn't I sell my penthouse when I had the chance?" But it's always the same old story: you are always cleverer in retrospect.

My life had been turned upside down; all of our lives had been turned upside down! I had always envisioned myself living abroad during the darkest months of the Icelandic winter, which is actually almost nine months of the year! During the bright summers I wanted to live in my penthouse. This had been my private dream and vision.

Unfortunately, someone else is living that dream of mine right now, since I was eventually forced to sell the penthouse for a much lower price than I could have before. I was angry at the time, but not anymore. Sometimes life takes over and forces us to comply. There was nothing I could do to prevent the chain of events that led to the economic collapse, just like you can't stop a volcano from erupting.

The consequences of the collapse were enormous in Iceland and it has taken us over eight years to recover financially. Morally and politically we are still dealing with corrupt politicians, but let's address that in the following chapters. You might have heard of Mr. Gunnlaugsson and a small company called Wintris?

Anyway, only two months after the collapse, I launched my new website on December 12th 2008. Right from the start, I set goals for this venture, and I have not only reached but surpassed all of them. Today I have over 44,000 registered users benefiting from my services, and that accounts for a huge portion of the Icelandic adult population.

A Strange Era For The Icelandic Nation

Even though chess is a fantastic game to prepare for life, life isn't always like a chessboard, where you can anticipate all the moves if you are clever enough. This last decade has been crazy here in Iceland, to say the least.

Who could have guessed that Jón Gnarr, a cutting edge actor and comedian, would decide to form an anarchist political party called The Best Party, win the municipal elections by a landslide and become the mayor of Reykjavík in 2010–2014? And not just that, but become both an effective and popular mayor as well?

And who could have guessed that the increase in tourism would continue for many years after the Eyjafjallajökull eruption, continuing up to this day to make tourism a major part of the economic recovery that Iceland is currently experiencing? The change has been monumental. Tourists used to be rare, so much so that nearly every one of them was asked the classical Icelandic question: *How do you like Iceland?* That's not the case anymore; we have gotten used to tourists and they have become so numerous that we can't ask them all!

In Iceland we have a saying: Fall er fararheill. It means that when you have a bad start, your journey will be great. That seems to echo well what happened here in Iceland: when we seemed to have reached the bottom, then Eyjafjallajökull erupted. But it came as a blessing in disguise.

Of course this surge in tourism isn't only a direct result of one volcanic eruption. Our fantastic musicians have made foreigners curious about our country; our filmmakers have impressed audiences around the world, often with eccentric and quirky films. Very recently, our national soccer team managed to sweep the world and draw attention to our remote island. And our rugged and pure nature, well, that in itself plays a large part and has attracted many Hollywood film crews, ranging from Noah to Batman, from Star Wars to Walter Mitty. And the latest addition to this cultural appeal is the Icelandic TV series Trapped that premiered in 2016 and received critical acclaim in many countries, including the U.K. and France. All of this has created huge interest in Iceland as a destination.

We have been through a lot the past few years. But we are resilient and honest people.

And in the long run, I think that always counts.

Messages From The Middle Of Nowhere

– Always follow your instincts and listen to your inner voice.

– Opportunities sometimes appear as problems.

– Sometimes it's enough to know your general direction – your exact destination will appear along the way.

– When the market is tough, new opportunities arise.

– Even losing a lot of money can involve a new opportunity.

– If you visualize a certain situation, be sure to involve yourself in it!

– Your friends get sparse when the ale runs out.

– Learn to read into the weather and understand the signs around you.

– When you have a bad start, your journey will be great.

And last but not least:

– You can't stop a volcano from erupting.

CHAPTER 12

HÚH! The Birth Of
The Viking Clap

The Ride Of A Lifetime

I will never forget a rough winter day and a crystal clear moment in 2009 that had a huge impact on my life. The weather was cold and windy; I stayed inside and was lounging under a blanket with my computer on the sofa, when I received an email from a friend of mine in Sweden with a website link and this message: "Check this out, it might be something for you."

I clicked the link and started watching a video from Brian Tracy, the legendary lecturer and best–selling author, with this compelling message:

"I want to introduce to you the biggest opportunity in the world." And Brian went on to introduce the concept of iLearningGlobal, describing in the most vivid terms this new approach on global learning. It was a subscription system, promising top-notch lectures from all the best speakers in the world. You could take seminars and courses, download e-books and audio books and even receive exclusive content. In 2009, this idea of online learning was just beginning, compared to how advanced we have become today with loads of material available on every topic imaginable.

And I got this fantastic feeling of WOW!

This is what the world needs! This is perfect for me!

Right away I watched another introduction from a guy I had never heard of before. He introduced himself as Bill Barton, billionaire, and he stated that he had never put his name on any venture in network marketing.

I spent the entire night browsing through all the material, literally every piece of information that was available about this new concept. I was so genuinely impressed that I couldn't wait to contact my friend Hulda to register through her.

I saw this as a fantastic initiative, not just for Icelanders but for all the world, since people in so many countries were running into trouble and having a rough time, needing something fresh and new and positive.

I called Hulda the following day and registered into this new and exciting deal, becoming one of the very first individuals in Europe to participate.

On The Brink Of Something Huge

Everything was just beginning. But that's OK, I thought to myself. So many reliable individuals have vouched for this network marketing company with their own name. It's solid as a rock, I thought to myself, even though I had always been reluctant to work with network marketing companies that hadn't reached five years in business. For me, that was a kind of insurance, even though of course companies and businesses can collapse whenever and however, no matter the amount of years they have under the belt.

So, trustingly I put everything in motion.

I went all in.

Right away I started benefiting from having participated in multi-level marketing previously, even though many years had passed since I turned to other ventures. My own constant reading on self-empowerment, personal development, and sales training also came in handy and since the core of iLearningGlobal was in my field of interest, I felt at home right away.

Within a few days I had scanned all my social groups and started sharing this opportunity with many people, telling them how brilliant the project was and how it would start rolling very fast. Given my credibility in Iceland, many of my friends and acquaintances were ready to jump aboard without much convincing.

With this enthusiasm I decided to stay true to my motto and give it my best. I had all the introductory material translated into Icelandic, proofread and supervised by text professionals and then I built a very professional website for the whole thing. I was on the highway to prosperity.

Recommending this online knowledge center wasn't a difficult process for me to do. I sincerely believed in the concept, and that's the best way for word-to-mouth to work. Before I knew it I was having weekly introductions for iLearningGlobal in hotel conference rooms, I was registering my friends abroad and they, in turn, were starting to register their friends.

The Word Spreads Quickly – All Over The World

Before long, my own network had reached 21 countries and was growing rapidly in several countries, especially Estonia and Latvia. I arranged for a special online meeting room where I could have introductions in Icelandic for Icelanders all over the world. We are not a large nation, but sometimes it feels like we have spread all over the world!

This success of ours was starting to be noticed abroad and Iceland was given the honorary title of 'the fastest growing country in the world', and my team and I were called 'Rock Stars of Iceland'. No wonder; the team was fantastic and we were on a roll, working superbly together and achieving real success. We were also having a lot of fun, which in my experience always leads to greater results, no matter what the project is. Naturally we had some naysayers around us, especially in the beginning, but as things started to roll more and more, it felt sweet to be able to tell people about our success.

We were doing so well that I was starting to have conference calls with the manager of the company and starting to cooperate with other prominent players in the field. One of them blew my mind when he said to me:

"Gunnar Andri, you are growing the fastest. If you keep up like this, you will become the biggest networker of them all. I'm sure that soon you will be making 100,000 dollars a month."

I took this as an exaggeration on his behalf, but nonetheless I had to admit that whenever I woke up in the morning and checked my status, new registrations had flooded into my network from all over the world, Thailand, Puerto Rico, and The Netherlands. And my paycheck kept getting bigger, even while I was sleeping. Iceland was becoming more insignificant for this global learning business, being a micro-market to begin with. But here I was, located in the middle of nowhere, feeling like I was conquering the world.

I tried my best to treat this success of mine like a submarine, sailing deep under the surface and below radar. Although incredible revenues seemed just around the corner, something told me to lay low. Network marketing is a tricky business, a bit like a bamboo tree. The roots can take a long time to become firm and fruitful, but when the bamboo starts emerging it only takes it a few days for it to reach its full growth potential. Similar principles apply to volcanoes. They can appear dormant for many years, but underneath you have a boiling and bubbling eruption waiting to happen in a flash and bang. When it starts, nothing can stop the volcano.

And in my experience, these principles also apply to success. When it finally arrives, perhaps after many meager years, you won't know what hit you.

The Final Night In Akureyri

Everything was going according to plan. I had taken a trip to Akureyri in North Iceland, since presenting an opportunity like this in person is always many times more effective than presenting over the phone or online. The conference room in Hotel KEA, the town's largest hotel, was packed with locals that were eager to hear about iLearningGlobal.

In Akureyri I did my usual presentation, explaining that ILG was a fantastic company and that we were the right people at the right time to take the leap. I got a great response from the crowd and many participants were already registering and listing up their friends and acquaintances in other countries. Some of them had their own laptops to register with, but others had to rely on the computers in the lobby and they formed lines waiting to register.

I felt great about all of this. I looked at all those engaged people that were willing to take the leap into wealth and knowledge. And I also knew that my own check would rise by a few dollars for each registration, resulting in even more registrations in other countries.

Ready To Reap

I had finished my presentation, so I went out on the veranda to light up a cigar to celebrate. Through the glass I could see a full lobby of enthusiastic new partners. Triumphant, I made a call to Konráð, a friend of mine who had successfully introduced ILG in Latvia. When he answered, I immediately said to him:

"Just think, Konráð, it's only a matter of months before we will become financially free for life. Next month's check will be sky–high. The growth of this project and its explosive power reminds me of an eruption. Even though the growth slows down, we will still be rich. No worries about money, ever again. That's our position now. Who would have thought? That in a single year we would have managed to return from a low point into full-blown riches!"

The phone was dead silent.

"Konráð? Are you there?" I shouted into the phone, looking at people in the lobby smiling and giving each other high–fives.

"So, you haven't heard?" my friend replied.

"Heard what?" I said.

"ILG is quitting network marketing,".

"Get out of here! I'm not in the mood for this kind of sick humor!" I said.

"Let me tell you, Gunnar Andri, I would never joke around with this kind of thing. I am not joking. They are closing it down," Konráð replied.

Suddenly I heard that the tone of his voice was dead serious. I was utterly speechless. My whole world was falling to pieces. Again!

"I don't believe this," I finally said, barely managing to stand. "I'll get back to you, Konráð, I have to tell everyone about this. They are celebrating right now! What on earth do I tell them?"

"I wouldn't want to be in your shoes, Gunnar Andri. But

there is only one way for you to handle this. Just level with them."

I walked into the lobby and the group immediately picked up the bad vibes. A woman asked me:

"Did someone just die?"

"No. Not quite, but please step into the conference room. We need to talk."

I plunged into the deep end of the pool:

"I have some terrible news. ILG just quit network marketing. You will get everything refunded tomorrow. I am very sorry."

Naturally, they bombarded me with questions.

"It's over? Why? How about you, will you get your paycheck next month?"

"No, it's game over. Completely."

It was a collective shock. Fortunately, the people were understanding and grateful for the fact that I had dealt with the situation face to face. After everyone was gone, I remained by myself, contemplating this new scenario. Just days earlier I had triumphantly opened a bottle of Dom Pérignon and smoked a Romeo y Julieta Churchill cigar while watching the amazing Northern Lights dance in the sky. Now I was staring into the abyss, no triumph, only shock and defeat. I stared at Akurey-rarkirkja, the high-rising grand cathedral across the hotel, looking at the snow falling, and I thought to myself:

"What does God mean by all of this? Haven't I been through enough? There must be some higher purpose to this!"

Immediately, a thought rushed through my head:

"This is clearly a disaster. But it will make the book even better."

Of Course This Too Will Make The Book Even Better

Right away I decided not to point the finger at everyone else or to blame Brian Tracy for how things went. I knew there had to be a good reason behind all of this, and later I got the chance to personally meet Brian and get a satisfying explanation. There is an Icelandic expression that we use when we need to recover, 'að ná vopnum sínum'. It means 'to redeem your weapons'. And that's what I decided to do, right away.

For me, the main lesson is this: You gain nothing from searching for a culprit. I am still a huge fan of network marketing, but the lessons I also learned are that you have to pick your partners very carefully and your risk is always bigger if you are dealing with a new company with no track record at all.

So, it was the end of the road for ILG and my general reputation in Iceland was on the line. I had to make the best of a terrible situation, so I went into crisis management mode. We had formed a great team of talented individuals, both in Iceland and in other countries, and I didn't want our collaboration to come to an end. Together we decided to aim for another network marketing venture that had just arrived in Iceland. I didn't know much about the product itself, but the quality seemed good and it was a reliable company.

We started calling our partners, first explaining the situation with ILG and then introducing the new opportunity. My phone calls went like this:

"So, this is the situation, but we have another network marketing project lined up. Are you in?"

If they replied with questions (what's this venture about and what's the product?) I replied:

"I don't have time to explain it right now, but let's just say it's all about selling tomatoes. Are you in?"

Incredibly, many of them instantly said yes, even if they

had no info about the product they were agreeing to sell. I felt like a captain on a fishing boat where I had the full and utter trust of everyone on board. It didn't matter if we were selling tomatos or tomatoes; many individuals were open for anything, following my lead and trusting my judgment. The business of sales is also the 'selling of individuals', meaning that for one reason or another, their trust in me was not totally lost.

If you can create a solid team that knows how to cooperate, success is always just around the corner. Our national soccer team was an example of this during the Euro in France 2016. But unfortunately, Iceland never really opened up to this new network marketing product and the balloon popped within months.

Frustration and disappointment.

Again.

This small flame of a business opportunity was nothing like the spectacular fireworks we Icelanders shoot up on New Year's Eve. It just went up, and straight down again like third-grade fireworks.

This marked the end of my career as a participant of network marketing. Would I recommend network marketing to others after all this experience? Absolutely. Jim Rohn once said: "Work full time on your job and part time on your fortune." For many people, network marketing is the perfect way to achieve this goal.

Sources Of Inspiration

Numerous people have inspired me throughout the years, both through their lectures and their books. Jim Rohn is one of these individuals, but I also recommend that you read the books by Robert T. Kiyosaki, Rich Dad Poor Dad and Cashflow Quadrant: Rich Dad's Guide to Financial Freedom. These are fabulous books that have taught me considerably. As mentioned earlier, I have been an avid reader of books on finance and personal development over the years, but one thing is for certain: I never lend books to people anymore. Why? The good ones never return to me, and then I feel like I've lost a great friend. I prefer to give copies of books to people that show an interest in my favorite titles than to let go of my own copies. It's impossible for me not to name a few books that have inspired me greatly through the years and have mixed well with the Viking mentality:

Think And Grow Rich by Napoleon Hill, *The Alchemist* by Paulo Coelho, *Start With Why* by Simon Sinek, *The Compound Effect* by Darren Hardy, *The Millionaire Mind* by Thomas J. Stanley, *Multiple Streams Of Income* by Robert G. Allen, *The Success Principles* by Jack Canfield, *The Millionaire Messenger* by Brendon Burchard, *The 7 Habits of Highly Effective People* by Stephen R. Covey, *The Power of Positive Thinking* by Norman Vincent Peale, *You Can Heal Your Life* by Louise Hay, *Awaken the Giant Within* by Anthony Robbins, *How to Win Friends and Influence People* by Dale Carnegie, *Chicken Soup for the Soul* by Jack Canfield and Mark Victor Hansen, *Eat That Frog!* by Brian Tracy and *Maximum Achievement* by Brian Tracy.

They all have different approaches and all of them deliver a powerful and valuable message.

Never The End – Always A New Beginning

And what about the network marketing adventure that went totally wrong? It wasn't the end. It was a new beginning.

For me, there was nothing else to do than to reach back into the bottom drawer and reconnect with my website, 2fyrir1.is. Maybe it was a misused opportunity? I hadn't been doing much for the website after having focused fully on ILG for many months. Nonetheless, it already had 10,000 registered users, which was OK, but nowhere near my expectations.

At this point in time, I set myself a goal. I wanted my discount club to have at least 30,000 registered users, and in the back of my mind I even had an extra ambitious goal of 40,000 users. That is somewhere around 15–20% of the total population. When I started talking about this goal to my friends and colleagues, no one believed in it, probably because Icelanders have never been much of a coupon nation. We have generally been reluctant to hand over a coupon to get our discount, unlike many other nations.

I had no money for marketing, branding, or advertising, so all my business deals involved bartering of some sort. I used all kinds of alternative ways of receiving attention, but I also didn't hesitate to do what we have to be able to do in difficult situations: Ask for help.

I called all over the place, approaching both friends and colleagues. I tried to be open and honest by first saying what I could do for him or her, and then asking if I could possibly ask for a favor in return. In most cases, it went really well, maybe in part because of our hectic economic situation where everyone had to use alternative measures to survive.

And voilá! I reached my goal of 30,000 users within a few months. And today the users amount to 44,000 on the site itself, and 40,000 on the Facebook page. I know it's a small market;

some people think it's so small that it would have been enough to shout '2fyrir1.is' out in the streets, but nonetheless I had to make an effort to reach my goals and secure my success.

The Complex Reality Of The Small Business Owner

Being a small business owner, most of the time you need to be everything at the same time: the manager, the marketing director, the sales manager, the salesman, the bookkeeper, the support desk service provider, etc. People tend to have this romantic idea of the life of an entrepreneur and small business owner. But the reality is endless work, sometimes 24/7, often 7 days a week, with the harvest often delayed.

During this time where I focused on my coupon website I also opened another site, www.happyhour.is, and re-designed and updated www.leikhus.is. Before I knew it I had accumulated thousands of emails that today are almost 100,000 emails from all these ventures, a pretty impressive yield considering how small our nation is.

All of this got me thinking really hard about my life and where I wanted to be heading. Did I want to be a large fish in a small pond? Or would I rather be a small fish in the ocean? If I wanted to take a new leap in my life, where could I find new opportunities? How could I work on a larger scale, being situated in the middle of nowhere?

I looked at everything I had experienced, everything I had built, from my extensive teaching experience, to my network marketing ventures, my sales experience, and my entrepreneurship concerning the website. This was me, this was what I had to offer.

And maybe I could offer it on a larger scale?

Through the years, my friends and colleagues had often asked me:

"Why don't you move your message abroad, teaching seminars and doing lectures? Iceland is way to small for you, Gunnar Andri."

And through the years, I have replied, truthfully:

"I am not interested in a life on the road, endlessly flying between cities and living out of a suitcase."

Nothing has changed in this regard. I still am not interested in spending my life on the road. But today, I don't have to. Today, I can deliver my message to hundreds of thousands of people online through different social media platforms. It's a fantastic and ongoing revolution, and I intend to take part in it hands-on for many years to come.

That Thing I Really Want To Do

In retrospect, I have done innumerable things in my life without understanding their purpose at the time. So many elements and experiences that just seemed trivial and even worthless. But now it seems to me that life has placed me in situations that made me capable of doing what I always wanted to do:

To encourage people all over the world to strive for their dreams and fight for their goals and never, ever give up ... even when the going gets tough.

Mistakes and defeats are the perfect way to learn to be successful. Failure is no big deal, as long as you rise back on your feet and continue. And remember: Your book will only get better. Your story will help you along the way if you allow it to become a positive experience.

Because of my own experiences with success and failure, after fighting fire and ice, I know for a fact that I can help people more than ever before in achieving their success. If you have failed and felt miserable, I can assure you that I have, too.

And if someone else has managed to find his success, then I can, too.

And so can you.

Our job is to figure out the essence of other people's success. Why have they become successful? What is their successful thinking? What are their successful actions?

Often we can mimic these actions and improve them to do even better. Why accept being good when you can be great? My point is this: *You can learn anything. Today, nothing is out of reach.* The Internet is a fantastic way to acquire knowledge and inspiring material and the same principle always applies:

Do everything in your power, always give everything you have, and success will follow.

Finding A Way To Meet Brian Tracy

This is what I did, not so long ago, when I heard that Brian Tracy would be visiting Iceland and giving a lecture. I had met him for a couple of minutes some years earlier, but I really wanted to meet him one on one, having already learned so many things from him over the years through his books and lectures. I wanted to meet him over dinner and get to know him. So, I arrived at this classical question of mine: "What can I do for Brian Tracy that will make him want to meet me for dinner?"

At first, I couldn't think of a solution. But then I remembered that I was acquainted with Brian Tracy's agent here in Iceland. I called the guy and asked him how things were going and how ticket sales were standing. He said that it was going OK, considering that it was Brian's 9th visit to Iceland, but that of course he would prefer it if sales were a bit better.

This was my chance. I knew that five attendees would get to have dinner with Brian, so I told the agent that I would be glad to help and that all I would ask for in return was admission to his seminar and his dinner event. I told the agent that I wouldn't charge a penny, that this was all I wanted in return. Of course, the deal was sealed on the spot.

To maximize success on my end, I used all my massive mailing lists and my websites to promote the event. I even re–directed some traffic from my own sites to a competitor of mine that was handling the ticket sales for the event.

The Dream Dinner And A Phone Call Of A Lifetime

We did fantastically and the event was a major success. The five of us went to dinner with the legendary Brian Tracy, and I even got seated next to him. There I was, chatting with Brian like he was just an ordinary guy, this legend that had impacted my life so much, without knowing it himself. Nonetheless, I felt at ease and I simply joked around, laughed and engaged fully in all conversations, without being star-struck by his fantastic company.

During our dinner we began talking about role models and I told Brian how impressed I was with Bill Bartmann, not just because of his catch phrase 'The Billionaire That Nobody Knew', but mostly because of his interesting life story.

Brian reached into his pocket and started dialing. Due to

some technical difficulties, his phone wouldn't work so I handed him my phone and told him to make any calls he needed. He started dialing, put the phone to his ear, and when someone answered on the other end of the line he said, loud and clear:

"Bill, hi, listen. You know, I am in Iceland and I am now having dinner with your #1 fan in the whole world. His name is Gunnar Andri and he is a lecturer. You should get to know him."

Brian Tracy handed me the phone. For a few moments I was completely speechless. You could hear a needle drop around the table. On my phone I had this hero of mine, Bill Bartmann. And in my phone I now had his private number. Now I was a little star-struck!

Our phone conversation was pleasant but short, but I will never forget this moment as long as I live. I had visualized this meeting with Brian Tracy many years before and now it had come true, but I had never imagined that in addition I would have a private conversation with my personal hero, Bill Bartmann.

You don't need to have a detailed plot of your whole journey, but you must visualize your destination and put in the extra effort to get a seat at the high table.

Later on, I was honored to write a chapter in the book *Against The Grain* that features chapters from Brian Tracy and many other prominent individuals. My chapter was called 'When The Eruption Starts, Location Is Everything', and it's the first chapter in this book.

Against The Grain went on to become a best–seller on Amazon. I can therefore already claim to be a 'best–selling author', although my greatest pleasure was to be included in a book with Brian Tracy.

The publication of *Against The Grain* led to extensive media attention, both in Iceland and abroad. I did various interviews with newspapers, magazines and even a television interview for a TV station in Belarus.

The Wintris Scandal

So often in life, everything hinges on your standing with your own views and convictions, no matter what. This may be challenging, but it's essential for your success – and for our success as a greater society. Especially when it's a matter of moral and ethics.

This is what happened when the Icelandic Prime Minister, Sigmundur Davíð Gunnlaugsson, was exposed in April 2016 as one of the prominent officials and world leaders that were found in the Panama papers and it became public knowledge that he owned an offshore company with his wife. This lead to public outrage and the day after the TV show aired, around 30,000 people protested at Austurvöllur where our parliament Alþingi is located. Just as in 2009, after the economic crash, people voiced their dissatisfaction clearly.

In an incredible week, Gunnlaugsson was forced to resign, mostly because of the pressure from the public and from the media outlets. The nation didn't trust its leader anymore and the entire government was in fact under attack since two other ministers also had connections to offshore companies in Panama.

I admire this kind of action, where people take a stand and defend their own integrity along with their peers. I believe that together we can change this world for the better, but to do so we must stand united.

One of the reasons I mention this is to emphasize how the Icelandic way of thinking is often entwined with cultural references. During these scandalous events, Óttarr Proppé, a member of parliament, famously said from the Althingi podium:

> "God bless Iceland and all that ... but
> trolls can take this government."

Yes, it's true what they say: The truth will always come out eventually. That's why honesty is such an important factor in a successful life.

Keep Your Dream Alive! Look Where It Got Our National Soccer Team!

Do you have a dream? Never give up on it! Anything is possible. The latest and the greatest example of this is the incredible success that the Icelandic soccer team achieved in Euro 2016. We were by far the smallest nation ever to reach the finals in this important soccer competition and just to make it to the final tournament was a huge milestone for Icelandic sports. And then what happened? In our first match, we drew 1–1 against Christiano Ronaldo and the Portuguese team! A few days later we got the same results against Hungary and at that point, anything was possible.

We only needed to survive one match to advance.

In our next match we were up against Austria, a team that many had favored to win the tournament. The match was really intense and at the very last minute our team managed a fast counter-attack that ended in an incredible winning goal by Arnór Ingvi Traustason! The game ended 2–1 and we were through to the next round – against all odds!

At this point in Iceland, everyone went berserk. This was such a dream come true, especially after all those years of struggle and hardship in our society. It was a redemption that we had yearned for.

But the adventure wasn't over. Far from it! We were still to face England in the round of sixteen. And what a game it was! England scored the first goal after only four minutes and their relief was obvious. The ice had been broken and they seemed to settle into a confident state. But only two minutes later, Iceland equalized! And after another few minutes, the Icelandic forward Kolbeinn Sigthórsson scored again! Happiness exploded and every single home in Iceland was screaming and shouting. For the remainder of the match, the English frantically tried to catch up, without success. The Icelandic defense line was fierce and managed to stop every attack.

The outcome: One of the most shocking results in the history of soccer when Iceland beat England 2–1, advancing to the round of eight! Not only had we made it to the final tournament, survived the group stage, and advanced to the round of sixteen, but now we had conquered one of the strongest soccer teams in the world.

It was the underdog story of the year, perhaps the decade.

And how did it end? Did we go all the way to win the Euro itself? Not quite. In the next match, we played against the strong French team and lost our first game of the tournament.

This concluded our fantastic journey. Our pride was bursting, our feelings exploding, and soon we will start the preliminary competition for the World Cup in Russia 2018.

Who knows? Maybe we'll repeat this incredible story, and even go all the way to the finals?

HÚH! The Viking Clap That Conquered The World

So this is how Iceland managed to use soccer skills to make history. But another star of this tournament was the now famous Viking Clap that our supporters used over and over again to express their support for the Icelandic team.

I'm sure you know it …HÚH!

If you don't, then please go online and find a video.

It was an amazing journey, especially the victory over England. Many commentators joked about this and said that 'little Iceland' had more volcanoes than professional football players, and they were right! But this only goes to show how far you can go with talent, humility and unity.

Talent isn't always what counts the most. Everyone can agree that many individual players of England were 'better' players. But spirit and effort can easily make all the difference. This has been proven over and over again.

One thing is for sure. All the Icelandic players had given everything they got, heart and soul, in all the matches in the tournament. They had a clear vision, supported by fantastic coaches, the Swedish Lars Lagerbäck and the Icelandic Heimir Hallgrímsson. They were fully supported by the very proud Icelandic nation, through every single step of this amazing journey. They followed their dream and their vision, and I sincerely hope that you will too. Success can become a fact in your life, whether you want success in business, sports, music career, the arts …it doesn't matter. With a fighter attitude, anything is possible.

Never give up.
Ever.

It's alright to take a break, but it's never OK to give up! If I could make a living by teaching sales courses in a nation of 330,000 people, then anything is possible. I've never used the size of Iceland as an excuse for not being 'bigger' in what I do. Besides, I am very grateful for having been able to do what I love for a living. In the words of Brendon Burchard in his great book *The Millionaire Messenger*:

"Never let your small business make you small–minded."

Do you have a dream? Never give up on it! Life has a tendency to throw us around and lead us astray. Just remember to follow the stars and listen to the signs. You just might be going in the perfect direction, even when you think you're lost. In fact, the ancient Icelandic magic stave *Vegvísir* on the cover of my book was intended to help the bearer stay on the right track during rough weather conditions.

And maybe the most important lesson is this:

Relax. Let down your guard. Enjoy life. Enjoy it some more, make yourself a better person, and then return as a better person with your sword and shield raised.

A Noble Name Will Never Die

The only true way to conclude this *Icelandic Viking's Philosophy For Conquering The Challenges Of Business And Life* is by quoting one of the sayings of the Vikings:

> Cattle die,
> Kinsmen die,
> all men are mortal.
> Words of praise
> will never perish,
> nor a noble name.

The best thing I ever accomplished in my entire life, apart from having my daughter, is never giving up on my dreams. I sincerely hope that you will do the same and that you will forever maintain a noble name through honesty and hard work.

See you at the top of the volcano!

Gunnar Andri Thorisson

Messages From The Middle Of Nowhere

– Never, ever give up! Your book will only become better.

– Never let your small business make you small-minded.

– Use the stars for navigation.

– Let down your guard and enjoy life.

– Redeem your weapons as soon as the battle is over.

– Visualize your dreams.

– Do everything in your power, always give everything you have, and success will follow.

– Ask for help.

– Make up your own mind: Do you want to be a large fish in a small pond or a small fish in the ocean?

– Choose genuine and healthy role models.

– Mistakes and defeats are the perfect way to learn to be successful.

– Why accept being good when you can be great?

– If you can create a solid team that knows how to cooperate, success is always just around the corner.

– Mistakes and defeats are the perfect way to learn to be successful. Failure is no big deal, as long as you rise back on your feet and continue.

– You don't need to have a detailed plot of your whole journey, but you must visualize your destination and put in extra effort to get a seat at the high table.

– The truth will always come out eventually. That's why honesty is such an important factor in a successful life.

– Do you have a dream? Never give up on it!

And last but not least:

– There is an Icelandic expression that we use when we need to recover, 'að ná vopnum sínum'. It means 'to redeem your weapons'.

The Essentials Of Quality Sales

If you make a sale, you can earn a commission. If you make a friend, you can earn a fortune.

Jeffrey Gitomer

To conclude this book of mine I want to give you my sales secrets. It's a simple, direct and proven process that I have developed for over 20 years, a little sneak peek into the art of achieving quality sales.

The Five Easy Steps To Quality Sales

In the **First Step** we cover the first sight, the initial contact with the customer. The initial contact is crucial, whether it is face to face, over the phone, or through other ways, like email.

In the **Second Step** we analyze the customer's needs and arrange for the presentation of our product, service, or idea.

In the **Third Step** we learn how to deal with negative responses and how to close a quality sale.

In the **Fourth Step** we cover the way we say goodbye to the customer or the person we are dealing with. It's a cliché, but it's true: A happy customer is the best marketing strategy.

In the **Fifth Step** we cover minor details that people tend to neglect: the after–sales contact that can secure a long–term relationship.

So, it's that simple. Five steps and guaranteed quality sales.

First Step: First Impressions

The saying is very true: You never get a second chance to make a first impression. If you start out wrong, chances are that the end result will also be negative.

First impressions are essential because, in general, we judge one another in a heartbeat. It's a fixed fact in human nature. We judge a voice that we hear over the phone, we judge other people, face to face. We judge based on the way other people dress, how they behave and how they sound. It's noble to do your best to minimize this, but the tendency is still there.

We make snap judgments. They might be horribly wrong, but we do it subconciously. And this matters because before people buy a particular product, service, or an idea, they have to begin with buying into you as an individual. This particular point I have been repeating for years and years.

People buy people.

It's that simple.

- People buy from either people they know or people they connect with.
- People buy from people they like.
- People buy from people they trust.

That's why first impressions matter the most. Always greet your customer like he or she is an important and welcome guest.

Words and Voice

During the initial contact, it's vital to show genuine interest in a person and use open questions to initiate the conversation. When you use open questions your customer can't answer with a Yes or a No. It's much better to use questions that start with how or why. The words we use are highly important, but so is our tone of voice. Be careful about the way you speak and try to talk to your customer in a natural and genuine tone.

"It wasn't what you said, it was the way you said it."

Do these words sound familiar?

Posture and Body Language

The second language of the salesman is his body language. I've read many articles on the matter, and for me, Albert Mehrabian makes the most sense. In his opinion, our daily communication, face to face, is 7% words, 38% tone of voice, and 55% body language. I'm sure these values could be argued, but my point is that much of what we are communicating to one another is delivered through means other than words.

Honesty

That's why it's so important to be honest, to generate a genuine interest in a person. Otherwise, people will see through you if you are not telling the truth. We, as buyers of products, often make our decision based on feelings and intuition, but we use our logic and our consciousness to back the decision.

The feelings that people experience don't necessarily stem from the words themselves, but from how they are expressed, and from their posture and the appearance of the salesman. That's why your attire is also crucial; it's a sign of what kind of a person you are, and clothes usually cover around 90% of your body.

Prosperity, friendliness, respect, trust: all of these are put forth during the first impression. You should, in fact, be making a new friend, treating your client kindly, being positive, speaking from your heart and finding something unique in him or her. This way you will make the atmosphere relaxed and your client will have increased interest in your product if your vibes are positive and genuine.

Never rule out a client in advance. Never ever do that. You will often find difficult or improbable clients to be the most fruitful.

During the initial phase it's important to reach the same level of your client. Try to mirror the client by using the same body language, the same words and discourse. Doing this will make you sound and feel more familiar and more reliable, because the client understands the words he uses himself. Nonetheless it's important not to assume that your idea of price range is the same as the client's. Prices are experienced emotionally, and people have different scales about fair prices for products.

Try to use humor in your sales approach, without forcing it. Positive emotions can have a huge impact on a sale. If you can make the customer smile, you can make him buy. In this regard, however, you may need to face reality. If you're not a funny person, then please don't try to be; just stay casual and pleasing.

Treat the customer the way you want others to treat you, and treat the customer the way he wants to be treated.

At the end of the day, most of us are fairly ego–centric. We like to talk about ourselves and we enjoy attention. When you see an old class photo, what do you immediately look for? Yourself. Always, it's a natural thing. Therefore, you must show genuine interest in your client, ask him about his life circumstances or be curious about something that is connected to him, or to his business. If you find a common interest, you will create a genuine and fruitful connection.

Start with friendly, informal conversation, like when you meet an interesting person at a dinner party or at a club. Just remember not to dwell too long on the chitchat; you can easily run out of things to say. And besides, you also need to get to the point.

You need to start selling.

All of the above sounds very casual. And it should be. But that doesn't mean that you simply show up. To make a good first impression, you need to be fully prepared. Can we get to know the client before we meet him? Do we have some information about him or her? Every little bit helps us to make a better connection.

Trust is a huge issue when you need to close a sale. If you come well recommended from the start, it will play a big role in the process. If the client has a high level of trust towards you, the quicker his decision-making will be.

Second step: Analyzing The Need

After the first impression, we need to establish a customer's needs. Selling isn't telling; it's listening and asking the right questions. This is a fundamental element of quality sales. If you are the one that is asking the questions, you are the one that is leading the conversation. And this we do to find out four fundamental facts:

– We ask questions to establish that our product matches the thing the customer is looking for.
– We ask questions to establish that the customer needs our product.
– We ask questions to establish that the customer can in fact use our product to fulfill his need.
– We ask questions to find out if the customer can afford the product, and to get him to agree on our price.

This entails that the product you are offering must be valuable for the customer and that he is willing and able to pay for it.

When you are introducing a product or a service, you need to paint a picture that the customer can visualize and see as a unique opportunity. The customer also needs to hear your words fully and understand them completely. And finally, the customer needs to start to feel emotions towards the product.

Speak the same language and follow the customer's lead. Here is an example where the customer says:

"I like what you are showing me."

To this, you should not reply:

"Yes, doesn't it sound good?"

A better way is simply saying:

"Let's take a closer look at it."

In this way you don't give the customer a way out and you keep speaking his or her language.

Let's take another example. If you try to tell the customer how great the product is, it'll be easy for him to dismiss your claim, thinking that you are simply being a salesman and trying to close the sale. But if you get the customer himself to say that the product is awesome, then it is his or her opinion, so it must be true.

Creating a feeling of ownership is imperative and will contribute to the closing of the sale. Therefore, it is always preferred to teach a customer how to use the product, rather than simply show or talk about it. The longer you allow the customer to handle the product and get to know it, the more you will increase your chances of closing the sale. Allow the customer to lead the way, to touch, feel, and try out the product as much as he or she pleases. Every second in this interaction will count.

Third Step: Negative Responses And Closing A Sale

Yes, it's true: Customers can be negative and it's easy to give up on them. But before I talk about the customers, I would like to address our own backyard: our own negativity.

If you want to master the art of closing a sale, the first thing you have to eliminate are the negative thoughts and excuses that you harbor deep inside your mind. You know them well, and I've heard them over and over again in my lectures and seminars. They kill good sales, and if you continue to carry them with you, you will never become a great salesman.

Here are a few of them:
– Of course I couldn't close the sale, the customer was wrong and he wasn't interested.
– I can't sell because my work conditions are poor.
– The price is too high.
– The price is too low.

In Iceland, we have some additional excuses, you might also be familiar with:

– I can't sell because everyone is so depressed about the bad weather.
– I can't sell because no one wants to hear a sales pitch in this great weather.

And the classic excuses:

– I can't sell because my boss is detestable.
– I can't sell because the company is no good.
– I can't sell because the company has been in the market for so long.
– I can't sell because the company is a new player in the market.

Excuses are your worst enemy because if you focus on them, they will only grow and grow and become even more relevant. Your attention refocuses quickly. If you are thinking about buying a certain brand of car, immediately you will start to notice this exact car wherever you go.

So, are you making excuses or making progress towards success? You can't make both at the same time. Therefore you have to be very focused, right from the first time you meet your customer. You have to have focus on your ultimate goal: to help the customer make a decision and to close the sale.

Remember Jeffrey Gitomer's motto:

If you make a sale, you can earn a commission. If you make a friend, you can earn a fortune.

In a quality sale, both the customer and the salesman come out on top. In each sale, the outcome is only as good as you are. Be the quality of your best sale.

If you want to close more sales, you need to improve yourself as much as you can, perhaps in many different areas. It takes effort to be a great salesman. You need to improve your first impressions, you need to improve your introduction, you need to improve your preparation, you need to improve your reading the signals of the buyer, you need to improve your reputation. You might even need to improve your time management and your goal setting.

In other words: You need to make an effort, if you really want to improve.

Many people tell themselves that they want to improve.

But only a few people actually mean it. And they prove it by putting in the extra effort.

The Negative Responses

After having worked in sales for over 30 years, in all kinds of companies, selling products, ideas, service, subscriptions, insurance, retail, books, selling to companies, selling to individuals ...after all of this experience, I have learned that negative responses from customers are basically always the same. This conviction of mine has been re-enforced by speaking to hundreds of salesmen from all over the world, attending seminars and reading stacks of books on the subject.

The negative responses are always the same, whatever the product or whatever the circumstances.

This is good, since you only need to learn one approach to respond to them.

What is the customer really saying when he brushes us off?

"I'll think about it."
"It's too expensive."
"I don't have the time."

The list goes on and on, but what is the customer really saying when he says "I'll think about it"?

Is he saying "Goodbye, I'll never see you again?" Is he say-ing "I'm not interested?" Or is he just saying "I'm not yet con-vinced?"

This must be our reaction, each and every time we get a brush–off. We have to estimate, in an instant, how warm the customer is on the scale of 0–10. Not only that: We also have to take into account when in the sales process he is trying to shut us down. Is it early on? Is it just before our meeting is coming to an end? Or when he walks out the door? Do we have a moment to tackle his response, even a few seconds?

Say we have a customer that is fairly positive towards our

product, because our initial introduction was successful. Everything seems to be going fine, but then he says he'll think about it.

What's the best response to this? To agree. We agree to his suggestion and say that it's a good idea to want to make an informed decision.

Our response puts the customer at ease and he puts his shield down. We continue to speak the same language and use the same discourse. And we might continue the conversation in a friendly and relaxed manner:

"Could I maybe ask you … before you leave … ?"

Or we say:

"While you are on the line, could I ask you if there is a particular reason for you to think about it? Is it maybe the price/color/size/delivery time?"

And this is very, very important:

After you raise this question, you absolutely must not say a word. You must allow this question to seep into the customer and you must allow him to answer, in his or her terms. We have created a space for an important answer, and whoever speaks first will lose.

The answer that the customer gives is our key to closing the sale. Let's say that he says the product is too expensive. This isn't a negative response; for a quality salesman, this answer is pure gold! Because we can't solve an issue unless we know what the issue is. If the price bothers the client, you are no longer facing an issue or a problem. You simply face a challenge: to convince the customer that the quality of your product is worth every penny.

An extra pointer is this: Ask the customer if price is the only thing that he isn't happy about. If he admits that it is, closing the sale gets even easier.

Incidentally, this process works for every conflict or negotiation, not just for sales. As I've said earlier, each and every one of us is constantly in the business of sales, each and every day.

Fourth Step: A Happy Customer Is The Best Marketing Tool

A happy customer is more valuable than the best salesman in your team. Word of mouth continues to be the strongest marketing tool there is. Therefore you must be careful how you say goodbye to your customer. It doesn't matter if he or she is leaving your place or if you are leaving the client's place; always make the last impression last. The same applies for sales calls, so say goodbye in a proper and direct manner.

A good speaker knows that at the end of the day, what people remember most is the final words.

Fifth Step: After Sales And Services

Reaching out again might be the most important part of a quality sale. And many salesmen simply don't think about this factor. After you have concluded a successful sale you should use the first natural chance to contact the customer again. This will strengthen the connection you have already made and create a future relationship.

Messages From The Middle Of Nowhere

– You never get a second chance to make a first impression.

– If you start out wrong, chances are that the end result will also be negative.

– People buy from either people they know, or people they connect with.

– People buy from people they like.

– People buy from people they trust.

– Positive emotions can have a huge impact on a sale.

– If you are the one that is asking the questions, you are the one that is leading the conversation.

– If the client has a high level of trust towards you, the quicker his decision-making will be.

– What is the customer really saying?

– We can't solve an issue if we don't know what the issue is. You have to ask the right questions.

– A simple aftersales contact can create a relationship that lasts a lifetime.

– Word of mouth is the strongest marketing tool we have.

– A good speaker knows that at the end of the day, what people remember most is the final words.

– A great salesman knows how to turn negative brush-offs into opportunities.

– Everyone is selling, each and every day.

– You need to make an effort if you really want to improve.

And last but not least:

– A happy customer is the best marketing tool.

Where to find me...

My homepage
www.GunnarAndri.is

Facebook:
www.facebook.com/GunnarAndriThorisson/

linkedin.com
linkedin.com/in/gunnar-andri-þórisson

Instagram
gunnarandrithorisson

Twitter
twitter.com/gunnar_andri

Made in United States
North Haven, CT
23 September 2024

57793664R00146